INFINITE Leadership

INFINITE LEADERSHIP

Drive a continuous improvement culture
and create excellence for everyone

KYLEE LEOTA

ISBN: 978-1-7638067-0-2 (pbk) eISBN: 978-1-7638067-1-9 (e-book)

A catalogue record for this book is available from the National Library of Australia

CONTENTS

INTRODUCTION

My journey into INFINITE leadership was not, perhaps, what you might expect. Rather than beginning professionally, it actually began personally.

In 2015 I left an unhealthy and unsafe marriage. In the end, it took the assistance of the police to get and keep me and my young children safe. Without focusing on all the gory details, leaving this second marriage was one of the most complicated times of my life. It was at that point that I became a single mother of three children, and it was also at that point I knew personally that something had to change for me.

I have often thought back to that time – about what was going on, what made me stay, what made it so hard to leave. Now whilst I do understand that my ex-partner's behaviour was his responsibility – I still wanted to understand my decision-making. How did I end up in that place, in the first place? Seeking an answer to this was probably the first time I can remember consciously choosing to do a deep dive into my thoughts and feelings. So I sought the help of a psychologist.

Of course, I'd seen psychologists before, off and on, for different reasons: when my grandfather died, a workplace bullying that sent me into early labour, and navigating post-natal depression to name a few. But when I was freshly out of this awful situation, I didn't have the right person to help me. So instead of leaning in to get external help, I dug deep into my own fierce independence. No doubt this was a result of trauma as well, this relentless need to 'do it myself'.

When I realised the support wasn't what I needed, I decided to sort myself out, myself. This was the first time that I remember consciously choosing a reflective practice to better understand what was happening in my world. This decision – though perhaps stemming from a place of trauma – was the step that I needed to begin to find my path to healing. And interestingly, where I really found something that made sense was when I started looking at the leadership materials that I had been learning about in my work life and started thinking about how I could apply them in my personal life.

Over the next 12 to 18 months, I started to look at all the different parts of my life through the leadership lens – what I was missing in my own transformation that kept letting me down, that kept me vulnerable to being led down pathways where I would second guess and question myself where I would allow people to get into my head and convince me that it was my fault, or that I should have done more, or any of those things. And I began to recognise the importance of my ecosystem – that is, the people that I surrounded myself with that would have my back, regardless of what was going on in my life.

Over the next two and a half to three years, I continued my relentless personal journey, all while working full time as a single parent raising a two year old, a nine year old and an 11 year old. It was tough, but slowly I got myself back.

I started to practise the lessons I had learned. That's not to say it was all easy from there. I was still dealing with fallout for many years, but instead of allowing that to dictate my life, I took the opportunity to learn and develop from it. I stepped into my own power, and I took ownership and responsibility of me and mine, and utilised the skills I had learned to become the leader in my own house just as I would in a professional level.

It was the lessons in leadership that got me through this journey, and I started to notice some patterns.

I noticed that it started with me, who my identity was at that time, or who I had created it to be that maybe perhaps wasn't me. I've been working since I was 15 years of age, and have had lots of different jobs from my very first ("check out chick" as we say in Australia (or cashier anywhere else)) to now, running my own practice. One of the challenges I found myself facing in each role is that I would attach my identity to the role. So when I was a deputy principal, I would wonder who I was if I wasn't an educator? And it wasn't until I had an injury in 2019 that kept me from working for months that I recognised how much my identity had been wrapped up in each role I played.

Who was I?

The first part of the pattern I recognised was that I needed to recalibrate myself back to who I truly was. I needed to lean into my emotions, stop burying them and ignoring them and try to understand why I was feeling the way that I was. To do this, I had to first identify and then move through my fears. I had to be innovative and recognise my own creativity, in what I was going to and in my strategies about moving forward.

I realised that even though it sounds counterintuitive, the best thing that I could do for myself was to serve others. So how was I doing that? Even though there was so much going on in my world, I needed to create my own influence and work through my own transformation and ensure the ecosystem I had around me was supporting me to get to where I wanted to go. Which was and still lays in service.

It was through this journey that I realised the power of the INFINITE journey both personally and professionally. I saw the benefits I derived from these leadership tools and I also gained a personal understanding of the challenges that many people faced when they were struggling versus those that seemed to sail from one success to the next. And one of the biggest of these is the inability to dig through the vast amounts of information out there, clear out the white noise and get to the information they really need, and then be able to take that information – the theory – and put it into practice.

And this is what I've developed with the INFINITE Leadership Model. I've taken the key elements of what people need to do to continue to reflect, review and recalibrate their lives, personally and professionally, and created a reflective practice that supports them to do that.

With the INFINITE Leadership Model, no matter where you are, no matter what's going on in your world, whether it be personally or professionally, you can move through this model to create change in your life. It works by starting from the inside out, and working through the different areas in your life where you aren't calibrated to who you really are or succeeding in the way that you should. Together we'll look at the areas in which you are already doing really well, and the areas where you might need to focus in order to get you back on your own INFINITE journey.

This journey is not easy, and it's not for people who are looking for a shortcut or a quick fix. If that's what you're looking for, this is probably not the book for you. When you start on your own deep dive on this journey, you will start to recognise that there are things that you haven't been doing, or that you've been doing at a surface level that you need to dig a little bit deeper on, and that can feel tough at times.

When I'm working with my clients, every step we take along the INFINITE journey is without judgement. So throughout this journey and throughout this book, I encourage you to treat yourself the same way. The world is judgemental enough. Being able to acknowledge and recognise places where you can improve without beating yourself up is the key to moving through this journey at a faster pace.

When you do notice yourself being judgemental of yourself and having trouble holding space as your own loving critic, I would encourage you to go and find someone in your ecosystem that can hold space for you to process your thoughts and your feelings. Just as I did at the beginning of my own journey, many of us fall into the trap of feeling that we need to do it ourselves, maybe because we've been let down, maybe because we've experienced trauma in our lives, maybe because we've felt it hard to accept that we might need help or to rely on somebody else.

The truth is that we all need support at some point, and there may be a point where you don't feel like you've got that in your world. And if that's the case, I would encourage you to reach out and find somebody who can support you through this journey, because honestly, you will need it to truly evolve into the INFINITE Leader that I know you're capable of becoming.

But this is a professional book, so why so many personal stories? The truth of the matter is INFINITE Leadership is both a personal and professional journey. In recent years, there has been a spotlight on being able to bring our authentic selves to work. If this is true, it requires more alignment between who we are personally and professionally. If one is off, both will be impacted, so creating synchronicity between both parts of ourselves is key to navigating the INFINITE journey.

Whether you're an aspiring leader, someone who has been in their role for a while looking to refresh their practice or someone looking to level up their leadership journey to a new role, if you're ready to get started recalibrating your life and your work to become a better, stronger, more impactful leader, a leader who is aligned with who you actually are, then this book is for you. Let's get started.

How to read this book

This book is designed to work for different brains! Which means for those who like to read from start to finish, great! The pillars of INFINITE Leadership are set out chapter by chapter and will take you on a journey that starts with the self and ends with leading others.

But if you prefer to pick and choose what matters to you most, each pillar is also a standalone chapter that has key insights and ideas on that topic that can help you no matter where you are on your INFINITE Leadership journey. At the end of each chapter, there are some reflective questions to help you build that reflection muscle. We know asking better questions of ourselves leads to better outcomes.

However you decide to read this book, I would encourage you to read the identity chapter first because INFINITE Leadership always starts with self.

Happy travels.

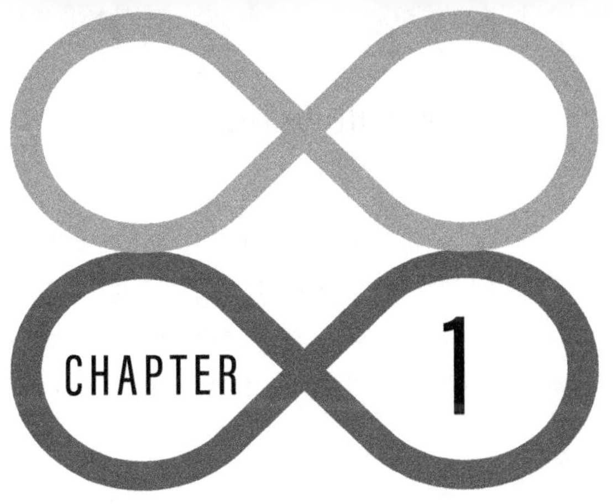

CHAPTER 1

WHY INFINITE LEADERSHIP?

We need leaders more now than ever. Events happening at a global level are causing so many issues, in many areas of life and work, and certainly in the leadership space. We have challenges arising in politics (just take a look at the American election), around new innovations and ideas and though we've got access to more information than ever before, we seem to be no further forward in the journey to real knowledge.

Atop of all this upheaval, we're also failing as leaders. And when we fail as leaders, we risk not just our own jobs and careers, and not just our organisation's ability to succeed, but society as a whole.

The Edelman Trust Barometer reveals a profound disconnect between leaders and the people they are meant to serve.[1] Year after year, it highlights how trust in leadership has eroded, reflecting a failure to adapt to the shifting expectations of the modern world. At its core,

---

1   Edelman Trust Institute. (2024). 2024 Edelman Trust Barometer Global Report. https://www.edelman.com/sites/g/files/aatuss191/files/2024-02/2024%20 Edelman%20Trust%20Barometer%20Global%20Report_FINAL.pdf.

this breakdown stems from a lack of transparency, inconsistent communication and a failure by leaders to engage authentically with those they lead. Leaders are expected to not only deliver results but to do so in a way that reflects integrity, purpose, and a commitment to the greater good.

What we are witnessing is a misalignment between what leaders believe is expected of them and what those they serve actually need. The gap continues to widen, creating a vacuum where mistrust thrives. Edelman's research paints a clear picture – stakeholders are no longer content with passive leadership or surface-level promises. Instead, they seek active, responsible leaders who drive meaningful change and take accountability for their actions.[2]

For many leaders, this growing trust deficit can feel like an insurmountable obstacle. But the solution lies in returning to the fundamentals of leadership – building relationships grounded in empathy, clear communication and an unwavering commitment to deliver on promises. Leaders must be seen as thermostats, not thermometers, setting the tone and driving change, rather than merely reacting to external pressures.

So, what's going on that is driving this trust deficit? What's going on with leadership globally? What's going on in Australia? And what can we do to stop circling the drain and make real leadership change?

What's going on with leadership globally?

Globally leadership is at a crossroads. The challenges of the 21st century are unlike anything we've faced before. Global crises are at an all-time high – climate change, geopolitical tensions and tech disruptions are

---

2   Edelman Trust Institute. 2024 Edelman Trust Barometer Global Report.

reshaping the way we live, work and lead. And the rise of populism and polarisation in politics has further complicated the landscape.

Leadership on a global scale is facing a profound transformation, one marked by increasing complexity, volatility and uncertainty. We are witnessing a pivotal moment where traditional leadership models are being challenged by rapid technological advancements, shifting geopolitical landscapes and societal demands for greater inclusivity, sustainability and accountability. The once-clear boundaries between sectors – government, business and civil society – are blurring, as the interdependence of these entities becomes more apparent in addressing global challenges like climate change, inequality and economic instability.

Globally, there's a growing recognition that leadership is no longer about maintaining control but about fostering collaboration, innovation and agility. Leaders are being called to redefine success not only in terms of economic performance but also in terms of social impact, ethics and long-term sustainability. Many leaders are struggling to keep pace with these expectations, clinging to outdated practices that prioritise short-term gains over long-term resilience. The failure to adapt is creating widespread disillusionment, as seen in the declining trust levels revealed in global surveys as mentioned above.

Leadership at this level is also grappling with the complexity of digital disruption and information overload. Leaders must now navigate a highly connected, yet increasingly fragmented world. The ability to inspire, communicate authentically and foster a sense of shared purpose has never been more critical. But the global leadership landscape is rife with inconsistency, as some leaders rise to the occasion while others retreat into protectionism, authoritarianism or stagnation.

Global leadership highlights a crossroads: leaders have the opportunity to reimagine their roles by embracing more inclusive, transformative, and forward-thinking approaches. Those who fail to evolve risk exacerbating the trust gap and losing their relevance in a rapidly changing world.

Today's leaders are being called on to make decisions in this increasingly complex and interconnected world. But the ripple effects of their actions can be felt across borders, institutions and their own teams – making effective and decisive decisions confronting. Leaders need to learn to navigate not only the intricacies of governance but also the deep divisions within society, and between members of that society and leaders in general.

A post-COVID world

We're now in a post-COVID world. Many of us just want to shake off the COVID period, move on and forget the challenges of a time when the world as we knew it turned on its head. But there are lessons to be learned, and repercussions still rippling through our systems. And this is particularly true in leadership.

One of the most significant lessons from the COVID-19 pandemic is the importance of agility and adaptability in business and in leadership. The pandemic exposed the soft underbelly of our systems – the vulnerabilities of rigid working and leadership structures, and the risk of top-down management approaches. The world soon realised that leaders must be prepared to pivot quickly in response to challenges – or risk being left behind.

The pandemic also underscored the importance of an empathetic approach to leadership. Authoritarian demand approaches simply aren't going to work anymore. During the pandemic leaders were called upon to guide their teams through fear, uncertainty and loss, and these lessons remain relevant today. Mental health challenges are on the rise, and working environments continue to evolve. The ability to lead with flexibility, compassion and a clear vision for the future is essential in navigating the complexities of the modern leadership space.

A global study in 2023 revealed that approximately 27% of people across 71 countries were categorised as 'Distressed or Struggling', while only 38% were 'Succeeding or Thriving', demonstrating little improvement since the height of the pandemic.[3] This stagnation indicates that mental health has not returned to pre-pandemic levels, with younger age groups, in particular, continuing to struggle more than older populations.[4]

Additionally, the economic toll of mental health disorders is alarming, contributing to nearly $1 trillion in lost productivity each year.[5] This is compounded by global inequities in mental health infrastructure and access to care, especially in low- and middle-income countries.[6]

Mental health issues, particularly among youth, remain critical. In 2023, organisations like UNICEF reported that nearly 35 million children, adolescents, and caregivers globally accessed mental health and psychosocial support services, which just serves to showcase the growing demand for mental health resources.[7]

---

3   Sapien Labs. (4 March 2024). The Mental State of the World in 2023: A Perspective on Internet-Enabled Populations. [Report]. Global Mind Publication. https://sapienlabs.org/wp-content/uploads/2024/03/4th-Annual-Mental-State-of-the-World-Report.pdf.

4   Sapien Labs. The Mental State of the World in 2023.

5   Karp, E & Yach, D. (2024). A Crisis of Our Time: Exploring the Global Rise of Mental Illness Through Economics, Lived Experiences, and Expert Insights. [Report]. The Aspen Institute. https://www.aspeninstitute.org/wp-content/uploads/2024/07/FLF-Crisis-Report-392.pdf.

6   Karp. A Crisis of Our Time.

7   UNICEF. (2024). Global Annual Results Report 2023: For every child, mental health & psychosocial wellbeing. [Report]. https://www.unicef.org/reports/global-annual-results-report-2023-mental-health.

Looking for more

Of course, the world has kept on moving forward, and there's no allowance for time to process the profound impact. We're still expected to pick up and keep going, despite having to navigate what appears to be a completely different world. In fact, it feels like the pace has gotten even faster.

The search for meaning in your work – for 'job satisfaction' – is becoming more prevalent as well. People used to get a job and stay in it for 20 years – even myself. For most of that time, I loved my job, but not all of the time. But the reality was that, at the time, you just got up and got on with it. There was no consideration about whether or not you were satisfied with your work. If you got a pay cheque and could support your family, then that was enough.

People today are realising that life is too short. They're looking for something more. I don't like the word *balance*, but I believe people are trying to seek a level of harmony in their work-life, in their professional and personal lives. I think they're trying to determine what this looks like for them individually.

Leaders are looking to make those same adjustments. But they're also facing a workforce that is looking for more. Leaders have always understood that we need both people and processes, but often they tend to focus on one or the other, and don't seem to be good at both. But in our new reality, more than ever, we must be proficient at catering to the needs of both.

Leaders often find themselves in their roles, not because they wanted to be leaders necessarily, but because they excelled at their previous positions. They were good at their technical roles. But excelling in a technical role doesn't automatically equip someone with the skills needed to navigate the complexities of leadership. Yet, our changed world demands more from us than ever.

Keeping up

The world slowed down temporarily during COVID, but post-COVID it feels like the pace has picked up, and then some. As the pace rises, so do expectations of what we can accomplish. How do we keep up? Morton Wierød, CEO of ABB, says 'remain curious, always be open for new things, for new trends, meeting people and listening to them with an open mind.' As leaders, not taking for granted that what we have learnt throughout a long career is necessarily going to be valid two or five years from now. As Wierød suggests, we cannot rest on our laurels. We need to be open to the continuous improvement journey, and embrace becoming an INFINITE Leader.

What's going on with leadership in Australia

Australia weathered COVID perhaps better than many countries, in some areas, but we still felt these changes keenly. And of course we're not immune to the rapidly changing world here either. What are the trends we're seeing in work and leadership? What are the positive and the negative pressures that people are seeing right here in our own backyards?

We're seeing budgets reduced. We're seeing people get laid off. But we're still seeing a huge need for stronger leadership. The economic pressures of a post-COVID world, coupled with the challenges of a tight labour market and rising inflation have placed significant strain on organisations across the country.

Despite these challenges, or maybe because of them, the need for strong leaders remains as critical as ever. This is particularly true as businesses navigate the return to in-person work and the demands of a hybrid workforce. Australia is also continuing to push for greater diversity and inclusion, sustainable work practices and the need for leaders to be more focused on social and environmental issues.

Post-COVID, the world has changed, as we've seen, but Australia has changed as well. The world has opened back up. People are coming back into the country, and even businesses who had to pivot rapidly to working from home arrangements, are pivoting back to getting people into the office.

There have also been some big changes in Australian leadership. Research by PwC highlights that hybrid working has transformed the workplace, providing a unique opportunity for businesses to rethink their strategies, and pushing leaders to adapt to new ways of managing teams.[8] As Australia pivots back to in-person work, many companies are experimenting with flexible work arrangements to retain top talent, while also remaining focussed on mental health and employee wellbeing, which have become critical concerns post-pandemic. This shift is not only about where people work but also how businesses foster engagement and performance in this new environment.

Return to office pressures, rising costs and workforce restructuring are forcing leaders to balance short-term economic pressures with the long-term need for sustainable, inclusive leadership. Leaders who can navigate these changes while maintaining a focus on innovation,

8   (2021). The Future of Work. Changing Places: How hybrid working is rewriting the rule book. [Report]. PwC. https://www.pwc.com.au/important-problems/future-of-work/changing-places-report.pdf.

employee engagement and social responsibility will be the ones best positioned for success in this evolving landscape.[9]

As Australia continues to evolve in this changing environment, the emphasis must be on developing leaders who can balance these competing demands while fostering innovation and resilience. And that requires leaders who can grow and develop with the changing demands. In other words, it requires INFINITE Leadership.

Why INFINITE Leadership matters

There have been many experiences in my life – like all of us – that I've had to navigate through. Upheavals, changes and disruptions are part of everyday life. But one of the biggest was one that I touched on in the introduction and that is experiencing, and ultimately leaving, a violent relationship and raising my kids on my own.

Of course, this is a single sentence that encompasses years of emotional trauma, healing and learning, and I still navigate everything that this entails. Over the years I've tried many different healing tactics, including psychology, working through self-help books and many more. But, as I mentioned previously, it was actually my lessons in leadership that were the biggest change for me in being able to navigate and pivot and eventually create the life that I wanted.

When I realised that it was applying the lessons of leadership that I had learned while in a corporate role into my own life that really changed my outcomes, I became passionate about sharing this widely. I have seen first hand that it can be game changing. And I think that we all lose

---

9   Hanns-Terrill, K et al. 'The Hybrid Workforce Post-COVID. *Executive Talent.* AESC. https://www.aesc.org/insights/magazine/article/hybrid-workforce-post-covid.

when we limit these lessons to people who are in the corporate world. This is why I've conceptualised the INFINITE Leadership journey.

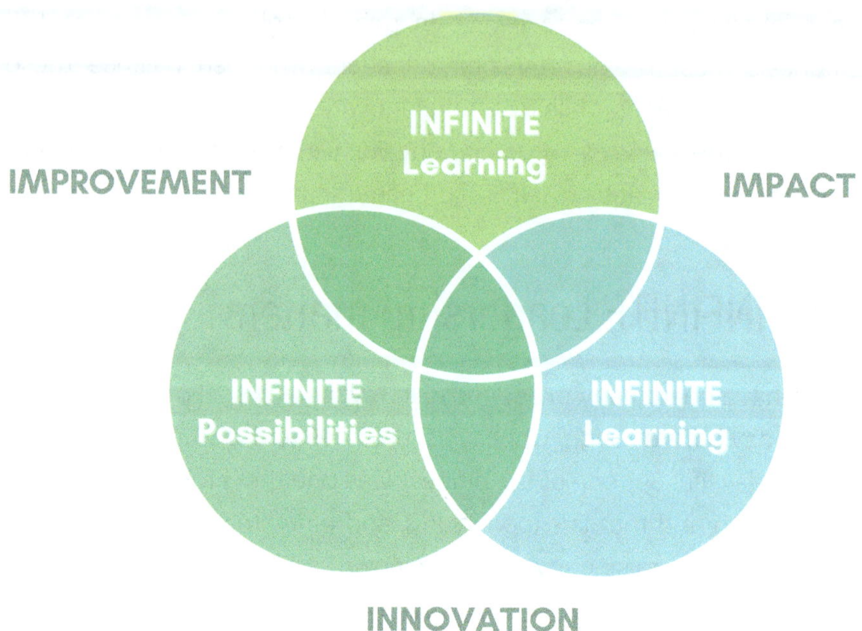

This INFINITE Leadership model encompasses how people can be empowered in the leadership space both personally and professionally, and it's what we will explore throughout the remainder of the book. It's by embracing the lessons of INFINITE Leadership we can see real growth in our lives. I feel this so strongly that I share these lessons with my own family continuously and I've seen my children benefit from the lessons I share, much earlier than I learned them. The goal is that despite the fact they will face challenges, they will have more tools in their toolbox for navigating them than I did. And this will ultimately lead to better outcomes, for them and those around them.

As I navigated (and continue to navigate) my own leadership journey, I noticed that there were many people who were also struggling in their leadership journeys. In fact, it was more common for me to find leaders that were leading poorly or struggling to lead than leaders that were doing well. One of the first leaders I truly admired wasn't always very popular with the staff, but his qualities stood out to me. He always put his students first and truly listened to what the staff had to say. Although he made his own decisions, he valued their input.

All these experiences highlighted to me the importance of the tailored approach to leadership development, including – and especially – leadership training. Too often, leadership training is generalised and lacks personal alignment, leaving individuals feeling they need to conform to a cookie-cutter model. But we're all individual human beings with our own thoughts and feelings, and we all operate in different ways. And so we need to have a model – the INFINITE model -- that will allow us to adopt bespoke leadership skills that are personalised and aligned to us. If we don't learn how to lead in this way, we will certainly fail.

My journey to leadership wasn't perfect. I didn't receive formal training until years after my first leadership role. It took deep reflection and a personal dive into leadership theory for me to recognise where I'd gone wrong, to identify the models that I had which might have been lacking and how I could fill those gaps and find my own feet in my own individual leadership style.

Today I recognise that my first years of leadership were not always my best for sure, and I reflect on that time, like I've encouraged you to do, without judgement. I found that there was a distance between where I was as a leader and where I wanted to be because nobody had shown me what it meant to be a leader.

I certainly didn't always have good leadership role models around me during my working years. But I can look back at the different leaders I've had over my working life, examine their different leadership styles and identify what I liked and what I didn't like. And I can still see these elements today in leaders that I work with. I can see styles that are more aligned to sustainable leadership practices and to the individual leader – and those that are not.

Often I go into organisations and when I see someone struggling with their leadership role, the CEO will say, 'But they should know!' And my first question is always, 'Why should they know?' In the leadership world we make an assumption that just because you have a leadership position, that you somehow acquired the skills and tools that you needed to become a leader. But that is patently not true.

Leaders become leaders for a wide variety of reasons. Maybe they're technical experts. Maybe they're the most senior. Maybe they share the same hobby as the boss! But whatever the reason you became a leader, if it's not working, if you don't feel successful, then we have to go back and look at where the gaps in your leadership skills might be. We need to reflect, review, recalibrate and reevaluate your own leadership. Then fill in those gaps. Then we do the process again. And again. And again. That is leadership.

When leaders have been put into a role and then are just required to 'sink or swim' (which is a very common outlook) they are primed for failure. And this failure does damage along the way. Instead we want to set up leaders (including ourselves!) so that when we step into a leadership role, we're stepping into a success story. We want to make sure it's as successful for those that lead as it is for those that they're leading *and* those that they're reporting to.

The goal is to get successful outcomes, and the best way to do that is to understand this INFINITE Leadership model, and move through it so that you (and all leaders) can, in real time, reflect along the way and continue to adapt, evolve and recalibrate. This will allow you to continue to level up your leadership during your leadership journey to what's required to lead well, and beyond. And this means that you're setting yourself up to be the best leader you can be.

So what is INFINITE Leadership?

INFINITE Leadership is a philosophy that recognises the ever-evolving nature of leadership and the need for leaders to be adaptable, resilient and forward-thinking. Traditional leadership models often focus on finite goals or endpoints. But INFINITE Leadership embraces continuous growth and learning, and it's this that increases the capacity to navigate uncertainty, which is more important than ever in our changing world.

We don't wake up in the morning and think, how can we do a bad job today, in our personal or professional lives. The byproduct of not having the right tools is that we can struggle more than we want or need to. We all want hope, stability, trust and compassion in our journeys. We look to our leaders to provide this to us, and we need to be the leaders that can do so. Along the way, we need to learn to provide this for ourselves, by taking the lessons in this book and applying them to our lives.

We'll delve into this in far more detail in the rest of this book, but for now we need to be able to see that this is the hook that can change our approach to a complex world – and let us function well as leaders. And that's why it matters.

Where to from here?

Our goal is to look at INFINITE Leadership as an evolution for infinite learning, infinite opportunity and infinite possibility. We have to explore the impact, the innovation and the improvement that can come when we take ownership of that journey. But there are many barriers that can hold us back from starting our own INFINITE journey. And we have to be aware and willing to overcome those obstacles if we want to embrace infinite possibilities. The next chapter will explore those potential barriers.

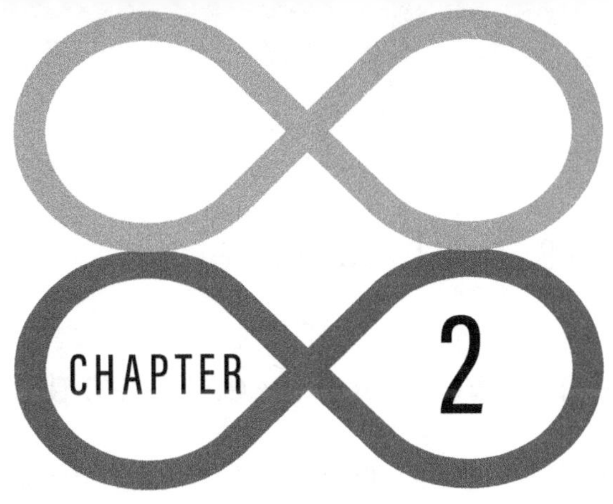

WHAT HOLDS US BACK FROM EMBRACING INFINITE LEADERSHIP?

'Unless you spend a reasonable amount of time proactively acknowledging and addressing the fears and feelings that show up during change and upheaval, we will spend an unreasonable amount of time managing problematic behaviours.'

– Brené Brown

The concept of INFINITE Leadership sounds great. It offers a compelling framework for navigating the complexities of today's world, and it seems easy enough – just keep learning! But, in reality, there are many barriers that prevent its widespread adoption.

The barriers that hold us back

Putting theory (even good theory!) into practice

Because we are right in the centre of the information age, our access to information is increasing exponentially. Currently, 328.77 million terabytes (1,000 gigabytes) of data are getting created every day.[10] That is an enormous amount of information that is quite literally in our pockets, and at our fingertips.

So as leaders, we can no longer say that we don't know. We do. Or we could and should. But we're still being held back, and the biggest issue seems to be putting the theory into practice. We can read, hear or be given lots of information, but we simply don't know how to apply it into our own lives to get the change that we seek.

Leaders often face the challenge of aligning these concepts with the realities of day-to-day operations where immediate demands and pressures can overshadow long-term goals. In other words, we're so busy doing the work that we struggle to think about the work and make changes to better the work. And the transition from a traditional, finite leadership role to an INFINITE one requires more than just a change in mindset. It means a fundamental shift in organisational culture, processes and expectations as well.

The inherent uncertainty in INFINITE Leadership can be unsettling when put into practice as well, for both leaders and their teams. The concept encourages experimentation and learning from failure, and in practice this can be confronting, particularly in workplace environments where there has historically been little tolerance for risks or mistakes.

---

10   Press, G. (9 May 2024). 'How Much Data is Generated Every Day (2024).' What's The Big Data. https://whatsthebigdata.com/data-generated-every-day/.

Leaders may struggle to balance the need for innovation and growth with the pressure to maintain stability and predictability – the status quo, in other words – and that can make it difficult to make the changes needed.

Your conscious and unconscious fears

When we're considering what's holding people back in general from stepping into their INFINITE Leadership, fear is still a huge challenge. People have come out of COVID more confused and more disheartened than ever. Mental health is a huge issue for society as a whole and it has only worsened since COVID.

In fact, one study done in 2020 showed that three-quarters (74%) of people reported that their mental health was a little (47%) or a lot worse (27%) since the outbreak of COVID-19.[11] After the upheaval of the pandemic, many people are simply more cautious and uncertain than ever before. For many, the idea of stepping into a new leadership paradigm – one like INFINITE Leadership – feels overwhelming.

Not attending to fears is one of the top three downfalls I see among leaders. Fear manifests in many ways, but in leadership it can be particularly paralysing. Leaders fear failure, fear making the wrong decisions and even fear losing the respect of their teams. After all, the stakes are high. And when fear is left unaddressed, it can lead to avoidance, micromanagement and stagnation.

As leaders, the longer we avoid dealing with fear, the more it will drive our behaviour and negatively impact our leadership.

---

11   (August 2020). 'Coping with COVID: the mental health impact on young people accessing headspace services.' [Report]. Headspace.org. https://headspace.org.au/assets/Uploads/COVID-Client-Impact-Report-FINAL-11-8-20.pdf

The role of fear in leadership

Fear is a funny thing. It's a universal human experience so we all have some fear to some degree. It's not an optional extra like a side dish we order at a restaurant. And fear can be useful for survival but when left unchecked in our work and professional lives, it can hinder growth and progress, or prevent us from innovating or making difficult decisions or even leading with empathy.

For leaders, we're not talking about a fear of spiders or heights. Because while those fears certainly exist and would perhaps stop you from seeking a job in the construction or pest control industry, they don't impact your ability to lead yourself or others to create an impact. Instead, some of the most common fears that hold *leaders* back are listed below.

Leadership Fears

- Fear of not being intelligent enough, smart enough or creative enough to lead effectively.

- Fear of failure as a leader, letting down the team or organisation.

- Fear of breaking the moral or ethical codes of the organisation or industry.

- Fear of not managing financial resources effectively or losing financial stability in leadership decisions.

- Fear of not being respected, valued, wanted or loved by your team, peers or superiors.

- Fear of rejection from colleagues, the board or stakeholders when making difficult decisions.

- Fear of not having the energy, stamina or presence to inspire and lead others to success.

- Fear of not being able to adapt quickly enough to changes in the market or organisational shifts.

- Fear of not creating enough impact or legacy through leadership efforts.[12]

For many leaders these fears are well below the surface, but they're still there, influencing their decisions and behaviours without them even realising it.[13] And when we don't recognise our fears, they can lead to flawed decision making, where we perhaps overestimate the likelihood of certain events, or make overly cautious decisions based on stereotypes or even have too much confidence in our own decision-making ability which means we ignore information that contradicts our own beliefs.[14]

This can happen to anyone. Because we all have fears. Any person or leader who says they've never felt fear is lying to you OR to themselves, or the much less likely but more worrying option, they're a sociopath. And because you're here, it's likely that you're looking to elevate your leadership, to become the leader that you aspire to be, and, as part of

---

12   These fears are a leadership focused version of Dr John Demartini's fear list which includes: 1. The mental fear of not knowing enough. 2. The vocational fear of failure. 3. Financial fear of poverty or loss of money. 4. Fear of losing loved ones. 5. Fear of social rejection. 6. Fear of ill-health, death or disease. 7. Spiritual fear of breaking the ethics of some perceived authority. Demartini, J. (2022). 'You can break through the 7 fears that stop you from reaching your full potential.' Dr John Demartini. https://drdemartini.com/blog/7-fears-that-can-immobilise-you-and-keep-you-from-being-a-leader.

13   Rathor. R. (3 August 2023). 'The Psychology of Fear: Understanding Its Impact on Decision-making.' *Medium.* https://medium.com/@ruchirathor_23436/the-psychology-of-fear-understanding-its-impact-on-decision-making-f40788f40ab4#:~:text=Fear%20can%20influence%20cognitive%20biases,can%20easily%20recall%20similar%20experiences.

14   Rathor. The Psychology of Fear.

that, find a place of fearlessness where your fears no longer define your leadership.

That's a fantastic goal. And fearlessness is part of INFINITE Leadership ('F' in 'I.N.F.I.N.I.T.E.'), as we'll explore later in this book. But it's important to say right at the start that fearlessness doesn't mean not having fear. Nor does it mean that we're pretending that fear doesn't exist.

Instead, fearlessness is about facing the reality of your fears, and how they're holding you back. It's being honest about what the true core fear is, so that you can first acknowledge and be aware, second begin to understand how and when the fear shows up as an unwanted guest and third, find appropriate strategies to move through the fear.

Growing up in fear

For most of my life (thank you hindsight) I grew up in fear. And while I can relate to many fears on the list, I also know through my own work that my primary fear has always been being unloved and unwanted.

There will be people in my life that may fall off their chair as they read that, because I do at times come across (I'm told) as a fierce, strong and unrelenting force to be reckoned with. And that might be true. But even when those behaviours did kick in they were really founded in fear. And this often meant that I was left scrambling and feeling (irrationally) that I was fighting for my life.

Our brains can be funny things. The vast majority of our interactions, situations and conversations are not life and death. But I've found that our brains simply can't tell the difference. I have lived through some actual life and death moments. And I've also had difficult professional conversations where it was challenging but I knew that I wasn't unsafe. Yet my brain elicited the same feelings in my body.

When we face something that scares us, whether real or perceived, our brains release stress hormones, including adrenaline and cortisol.[15] These are designed to prepare you for a threat, even if you aren't actually facing one. But these hormones then cause your blood pressure to rise, your heart rate to increase and your breath to come faster. Because blood flow also increases, you can feel a jittery energy in your limbs, and your ability to make logical decisions is impacted as you seek to do things too quickly and impulsively.[16]

So despite your brain knowing that you're physically safe, when you feel fears as a leader (and you will), you may feel these unconscious physical responses.

Your personality impacts your fears

Interestingly our fears can also be tied to our personality types. The Enneagram is a popular model for understanding human behaviour. It sets out nine core fears that can influence how we lead and interact with others.[17]

Type 1: Fear of being bad. This is the fear of being bad, wrong, unethical, immoral, incorrect, inappropriate or evil.

Type 2: Fear of being unwanted or unloved. This is the fear of being unloved, unwanted, not needed, not appreciated or needy.

15   Rathor. The Psychology of Fear.

16   Sikora, Z. (October 2020). '5 Things You Never Knew About Fear.' Northwestern Medicine. https://www.nm.org/healthbeat/healthy-tips/emotional-health/5-things-you-never-knew-about-fear#:~:text=Fear%20Is%20Physical&text=Stress%20hormones%20like%20cortisol%20and,or%20run%20for%20your%20life.

17   (18 May 2022). 'Enneagram Core Fears' Enneagram Explained. https://enneagramexplained.com/enneagram-core-fears/.

Type 3: Fear of being worthless or not admired. This is the fear of being worthless, a failure, not valued, not admired, not successful or inefficient.

Type 4: Fear of being insignificant or having no meaning. This is the fear of not having any significance or identity, or being common, defective or flawed.

Type 5: Fear of being overwhelmed. This is the fear of being incompetent, incapable, unknowledgeable, helpless, ignorant, overwhelmed and invaded.

Type 6: Fear of being without support or security. This is the fear of being without support, without guidance, without security, or being alone or abandoned.

Type 7: Fear of being deprived or trapped in emotional pain. This is the fear of being deprived, trapped in emotional pain, bored or limited.

Type 8: Fear of being controlled or powerless. This is the fear of being controlled, harmed, powerless, weak, vulnerable or manipulated.

Type 9: Fear of separation or loss of connection with others. This is the fear of being separated, being at a loss with others, having conflict or tension or being shut out or overlooked.[18]

Understanding these core fears can help you identify the root of the fears that might impact your own leadership. They can also give you insight into how these fears manifest in your leadership style, so you can address them head on.

---

18   Enneagram Core Fears.

The Upper Limit Problem – self-sabotage in leadership

Psychologist Gay Hendricks introduced the concept of the upper limit problem (ULP).[19] This describes how individuals often unconsciously self-sabotage when they reach new levels of success or happiness.[20]

ULP occurs because we all have an internal threshold for how much success, love and joy we feel we deserve. When we reach that threshold, our subconscious mind breaks in with a series of unpleasant or disruptive thoughts to bring us back down to our 'comfortable' level – or back down to our threshold. So our ULP is underpinned by hidden barriers based on fears and false beliefs and these are then manifested in our work and personal lives through destructive habits.[21]

How do we know when we're self-sabotaging because of the upper limit problem? Ask yourself these questions:

1. Are you deflecting praise?
2. Are you downplaying wins?
3. Are you avoiding opportunities?
4. Are you staying in your comfort zone?
5. Are you avoiding taking on bigger responsibilities?
6. Are you holding back from voicing your ideas?
7. Do you believe it's too good to be true?
8. Do you prioritise other people's opinions over your own?
9. Are you settling for less so you don't make others uncomfortable?
10. Are you making excuses to avoid stepping into the spotlight?

Which of these resonate with you?

---

19 Hendricks, G. (2010). *The Big Leap: Conquer Your Hidden Fear and Take Life to the Next Level.* HarperCollins US.

20 Hendricks. The Big Leap.

21 Hendricks. The Big Leap.

Identifying your own fears and self-sabotaging behaviours

Let's take a moment to think about your own fears. Out of the leadership fears listed above, which were the ones that you most identified with? What are the top three?

List them in the table below.

Now take a look at the nine Enneagram core fears. Which of these did you relate to? It could have been just a few, or quite a few (I've felt all of them at various times in my life or career). Now choose the top two, and list them in the table below.

Finally, let's review the upper limit problem. Which of those questions did you most identify with? Again, find the top three and list them in the table below.

Fear	Rank	How it shows up	What happens
Leadership Fears	1. 2. 3		
Enneagram 9 Core Fears	1. 2. 3		
Upper Limit Problem	1. 2. 3		

Once you've named the fears and self-sabotaging thoughts, spend some time thinking about how they show up in your daily life, especially as a leader. Then think about what happens when they do show up. What are the results and outcomes, negative and positive? This will help you start to see more clearly your own fears and the impacts they have on your own leadership. This serves as a great starting point for sustainable change.

How do we know when fear is in the driver's seat?

When we know what to look for, it can become quite easy to understand when fear is in the driver's seat because it will show up in your behaviour.

- Perhaps you notice, or you've been told, that you micro-manage your staff even if it's only when you're stressed. The fear here is of losing control or appearing incompetent.

- Perhaps people see you as intimidating. You may fear being vulnerable or appearing as weak.

- Perhaps you struggle to meet deadlines. You might be carrying a fear of failure or of not being good enough.

- Perhaps you're delivering a lower standard of work than you're capable of. The fear here is of rejection or inadequacy.

- Perhaps you're an indecisive leader. You might fear making the wrong decision.

- Perhaps you're not able or are unwilling to get close to your team. The fear here might be the fear of not being wanted or valued by your team.

- Perhaps you don't hold people accountable. The fear here is the fear of not being liked.

If you relate to any of these fears, you aren't the only one. Some of these fears impacted me as a leader as well. And some still do. Becoming an INFINITE Leader certainly doesn't mean you don't have fears – but you do need to learn the skills to move through them if your goal is INFINITE Leadership.

How to consciously move through fear

You need a way to move through fear consciously so it doesn't hijack you unconsciously. One way to move through fear to become the INFINITE Leader you need to be is via F.E.A.R.

> **F – Face it.** Name it (what is the situation?), describe it, explain it. Why is it driving fear in you? Name the actual fear as well.

> **E – Evaluate.** What information would you need to remove the fear? What is in your control regarding this situation?

> **A – Act.** Are you focussing on the things that you can control? Take action based on the things you can.

> **R – Reframe.** Has the fear subsided? Has it changed? What do you need to be able to reframe to be able to move forward?

F - face it

E - evaluate

A - act

R - reframe

Ask yourself these questions and take some time to think about what's working well and what's not. Consider what you can reduce or eliminate in your life to allow you to work on your leadership fears, then act. Review, conduct your own evaluation (without judgement) and take steps to better manage those fears and your responses.

Most importantly, continue to reflect, review and recalibrate (more on this in the next chapter!), remembering that the act of fearlessness is not to stop doing things because of fear, but it is to move productively through fear to the other side.

A lack of leadership preparation

Along with putting theory into practice and moving through our fears, another thing that can hold us back from becoming INFINITE Leaders, is the fact that we're not actually prepared to be leaders.

As we touched on in the last chapter, many leaders find themselves in leadership roles not because they aspired to have power or authority, but because they excelled at what they did. For these leaders, leadership is more of a calling than a conscious decision. So many leaders find themselves thrust into leadership without the necessary skills to navigate the complexities that leadership demands at higher levels. And even with passion about the work, these leaders can find themselves lost when it comes to leading others.

Often these leaders might feel a sense of imposter syndrome. They may question their own abilities because they lack the foundational skills for leadership. Their feelings may be exacerbated because they (like those that hired or promoted them) assume that leadership skills will develop naturally over time. Unfortunately that's generally not the case.

Leaders who find themselves feeling unprepared for their leadership roles are at risk of not being able to have the impact they are looking for. They may not be able to manage their teams effectively or implement strategies that align with the evolving needs of the team or the organisation. And leaders that are not prepared are at a much higher risk of leadership burnout and turnover.

A lack of preparation leads to a lack of confidence that undermines your ability to lead and holds you back from becoming the INFINITE Leader you want to be.

Getting in your own way

Another challenge that leaders face is the fact that many people get in their own way – and they aren't self-aware enough to get out their own way. There's a great analogy attributed to American coach, Jim Kwik that says, 'If an egg is broken from the outside, life ends, but if it's broken from the inside, life begins.' What this shows is the idea that great things often start from within, and that's why developing self-awareness is critical to overcoming your obstacles in leadership.

But self-awareness isn't always easy and it's common for leaders to unintentionally block progress or get in their own way, when they aren't self-aware. They're so focused on external goals that they neglect to examine their internal patterns and behaviours and make the changes they need. When you fail to reflect as a leader, you can become rigid, clinging to old habits and processes that no longer serve your team or organisation.

I had a leader who was phenomenal at times, but when the organisation, clientele and culture changed, her reluctance to adapt caused significant problems. She struggled to separate her self-worth from the processes she had created years earlier. And while those processes had been effective at the time, she couldn't see that they no longer served the evolving needs of the organisation. Her unwillingness to recognise the changes needed led to many talented staff members jumping ship. In the end, her attachment to outdated methods became a barrier to her ability to lead. And she simply couldn't see it.

To overcome this barrier, leaders need to embrace continuous self-reflection and be open to feedback from others (cornerstones of the INFINITE Leadership journey). You have to be able to question your assumptions, challenge your biases and remain flexible. These are key to adapting to the inevitable changes that will come your way, and stop being held back from developing your own INFINITE Leadership capabilities.

Inability to recognise intention versus impact

One last challenge that we may face as leaders, and that can hold us back from becoming INFINITE Leaders, is recognising the difference between intention and impact.

As leaders we generally have the best of intentions. We want our teams and organisations to do well. But we can also find ourselves struggling to separate our 'intentions' from the actual outcomes of our actions. We may mean well, but if the impact of what we do when we lead doesn't align with our intentions, it can harm our teams and the organisation as a whole.

Instead of digging your heels in when the outcomes don't come out the way you want – saying, 'but we were *trying* to achieve X or Y' – take some time to think about what the misalignment is. This is your opportunity to reflect, repair and realign with the goals that you set out to achieve.

Ready to reflect, recalibrate and evolve?

In this chapter, we explored the barriers that prevent leaders from fully embracing INFINITE Leadership. Fear is the most significant factor that holds us back, influencing decisions, behaviours and our overall leadership effectiveness. But as leaders we can also struggle with putting theory into practice, getting in our own way, seeing the true impact of our actions despite our intentions and getting support when we're not prepared to be leaders (and that's probably all of us!).

But we can overcome each of these and become INFINITE Leaders. In the next chapter we'll dive into how to adopt the reflective practice that is the cornerstone of the INFINITE Leadership journey. When we adopt this practice we'll learn how to recalibrate and evolve so we're always moving forward, learning from our experiences and becoming the best leaders we can be.

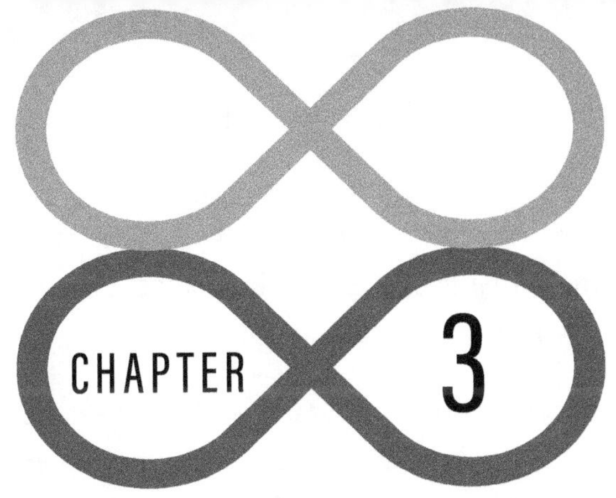

EMBRACING YOUR REFLECTIVE PRACTICE

*'Reflection is one of the most underused
yet powerful tools for success.'*

– Richard Carlson

What is the solution to the leadership challenges that we're facing, both individually and globally? What is the solution that will see us overcoming our fears and becoming INFINITE Leaders? How do we fix something that seems unfixable?

The truth is, no matter what role, what position you aspire to, or what kind of leader you strive to be, you need to have a strong reflective practice. This means that you must be able to acknowledge with honesty, authenticity and a level of self-consciousness where you are right now, and what you need to do to get to the next level. This is true whether you're looking at your own individual leadership journey or the overall organisational leadership. A strong reflective practice encompasses more than just theory. It immerses itself in action-taking to get to the next level.

That's because leadership is not static – it's an evolution. Every new role, every change that you face in your industry or organisation and every insight you learn about yourself requires an evolved version of who you are. You can't expect to succeed when facing these changes if you remain the same.

The INFINITE Leadership model embraces this concept of change. It's a continuous learning process that starts with accepting where you are, acknowledging what you're doing well and reflecting on what you can do better. This is the process of peeling back the onion's layers, so to speak!

At its core, INFINITE Leadership always starts with self-reflection. What is the outcome I want to achieve? How am I contributing to or hindering that process? What do I need to take ownership of, and what should I release? These questions are essential in understanding your role as a leader. So to start on our journey to INFINITE Leadership, we start with adopting a reflective process.

Your reflective process

The idea that we must continuously improve as leaders is something that has been embraced by high-performing corporations for many years. The original philosophy – known as kaizen – is a management methodology developed by the Toyota Motor Corporation in Japan.[22]

---

22   Hargrave, M. (27 February 2024). 'Kaizen: Understanding the Japanese Business Philosophy.' Investopedia. https://www.investopedia.com/terms/k/kaizen. asp#:~:text=Kaizen%20is%20a%20Japanese%20term,a%20gradual%20and%20 methodical%20process.

It is 'the quest for continuous improvement' and is one of the core principles within the value premise of that corporation and many others.

So what does kaizen mean? It means that leadership learning is not a one-and-done model. It is about cumulative growth in incremental steps rather than one breakthrough moment. When you adopt kaizen you're constantly evaluating where you are, what's working and what's not and taking incremental steps to improve your position. And you never stop this process. This is also INFINITE Leadership.

A great example of this is the story of the British Cycling Team, which, led by Sir Dave Brailsford, began focusing on improving by 1% at a time rather than trying to achieve huge improvements all at once.[23] He called this 'the aggregation of marginal gains' and it was an approach that saw the team searching for a tiny margin of improvement in everything that they did.[24] So they began making small adjustments such as redesigning more comfortable bike seats, wearing electrically heated overshorts that helped the team maintain the ideal muscle temperature when riding and switching to indoor racing suits which were lighter and more aerodynamic.[25]

What this led to was a team that won seven out of 10 medals at the 2008 Beijing Olympics and again at the 2012 London Olympics,[26] followed by winning six out of seven Tour de France races between 2012 and

---

23 Harrell, E. (31 October 2015). 'How 1% Performance Improvements Led to Olympic Gold.' *Harvard Business Review.* https://hbr.org/2015/10/how-1-performance-improvements-led-to-olympic-gold.

24 Slater, M. (8 August 2012). 'Olympics Cycling: Marginal Gains Underpin Team GB dominance.' BBC. https://www.bbc.com/sport/olympics/19174302.

25 Slater. Olympics Cycling: Marginal Gains Underpin Team GB dominance.

26 Harrell. How 1% Performance Improvements Led to Olympic Gold.

2018.[27] An incredible improvement that came from small, incremental improvements.

Making your green, greener

Of course it's easy to see how the reflective practice (kaizen you can call it or continuous improvement) can make an incredible difference for elite athletes where everyone is a world-class performer anyway. But what about other industries? It's not often as easy to see how this practice might work in the corporate or business world. But it certainly does.

When I was an educational leader, we had data sets that would come out regularly, that were designed to ascertain the level of our school's performance. The computer analysis would work its magic, take each school's data, compare it to key performance data and then identify where you were operating. You might end up identified as in the red zone, which meant things were not great and you needed to improve drastically. Or you might end up in the yellow zone, which meant you were doing better but still had improvements to make. Or you might end up in the green, which meant you were achieving high outcomes compared to the performance data. If you ended up in a sea of red, you knew an uncomfortable conversation wasn't too far away.

Obviously, when you were in the red or yellow zones there was a lot of work to be done to bring your school up to the green zone, and there was a huge risk of burnout for the individuals involved, both the staff and the leaders. There was an additional challenge in the yellow zone where the people involved – who were likely very tired from the work gone in to leverage up from the red zone – would just accept the yellow assignment, making excuses about their school environment and

---

27   Wood, R. (2024). 'Tour de France Winners List.' Topend Sports Website, first published May 2010. https://www.topendsports.com/events/tour-de-france/winners-list.htm.

believing that they could stay in their zone of competence, and accept that this was good enough. For some, this data could provide a sense of 'this is as good as it gets' or even lead to complacency from a sense of lost hope. Those individuals would feel that it didn't matter what they did, the yellow zone was where they would always be.

But another, even bigger, risk was actually for the schools that were performing well enough to be in the green zone. These are schools that were actually doing really well. Their data sets looked like a sea of green, and these 'leafy greens' as we affectionately termed it were the schools that were often in high socioeconomic areas, with associated high standards and high expectations.

The challenge for these schools was how to make the green greener.

It was challenging because usually these schools were already performing at the top end of the data set. It might have been easy for them to just take their foot off the pedal and coast. But true success is about continuing to drive excellence and performance, rather than settling for the current standards – even if you're already leading the pack. And so they looked around to find the places where improvements could still be made – and they made those incremental improvements.

This is how we need to approach our leadership as well.

How does a reflective practice work?

Metacognition is thinking about thinking. It's actually defined as 'knowledge and understanding of your own thinking'[28], and our reflective practice is essentially that. It's thinking about what we're thinking (and so how we're acting and reacting) in our leadership. And it's critical for

---

28 Cambridge. (n.d.). Metacognition. In dictionary.cambridge.org. https://dictionary.cambridge.org/dictionary/english/metacognition.

leaders who want to build a reflective practice. Hindsight really *is* a beautiful thing because it's after the fact that we have time to really get clarity on a situation. The emotion of the moment has passed and it's easier to see what we maybe should have or could have done, or even what we would do differently next time. It just gives you time to think about and process the information more clearly.

Of course, like everything in life, reflection is a skill that requires practice. It's like a muscle, and over time, and with use, it becomes stronger, faster and more skilful. So, just like any skill, the more you practice it, the better you become at it. And the greater our skills the more we're able to reflect and embrace the insights that come from that self-reflection.

The goal is to hopefully, one day, be able to do this self-reflection in real time as the situation is happening. This gives you a chance to respond differently when the situation needs it, rather than having a post-event dissection which will only allow you to prepare to be better next time (although this is certainly still well worth doing!).

When we're able to use our reflection skills during a situation that calls for a change in our behaviour, this ensures we're far more likely to get a favourable outcome. But if we keep falling back into the same patterns of behaviour continuously, we might expect to see different results, but we won't.

It's tricky to reflect when the situation is occurring, primarily because it's far too easy to get hijacked by our emotions in the heat of the moment. This is true for all humans, not just you and me, and certainly not just leaders. It's sometimes referred to as the 'amygdala hijack' which is when strong emotions take over the thinking part of your brain, leaving you to act in ways that you may regret later.[29]

---

29 Pederson, T. (14 October 2021). 'All About Amygdala Hijack.' PsychCentral. https://psychcentral.com/health/amygdala-hijack.

In order to embrace our INFINITE Leadership, we need to undertake a constant cycle of self-reflection, skills adaptation and action-taking. This will allow us to recognise the distance travelled, validate our own growth and stay motivated for the journey ahead.

To truly embody INFINITE Leadership, you must commit to this constant cycle of self-reflection. You must be willing to reflect, adapt and act. It's this ongoing process that will allow you to navigate the complexities of leadership and make sure you're always evolving as both a leader and an individual. And don't forget to celebrate the successes along the way.

What's next?

The remainder of this book is dedicated to your INFINITE Leadership journey. It embraces the practical 'how' of creating a reflective practice which overarches all the other elements of INFINITE Leadership. Our INFINITE Leadership journey will follow the path set out below, delving into each of the topics to enlighten our leadership and even our own lives on a personal level.

- **I** – Identity
- **N** – Nurturing
- **F** – Fearlessness
- **I** – Innovation
- **N** – Nobility
- **I** – Influence
- **T** – Transformation
- **E** – Ecosystem

Each of these plays an important part in becoming an INFINITE Leader. Through the following chapters we'll dive into each one, finding the insights and understanding that will help us shed the things we need to shed, and embrace the things we need to embrace to become the leaders we want to be.

*'I don't fix my problems. I fix my thinking and
then my problems fix themselves.'*

– Louise Hay

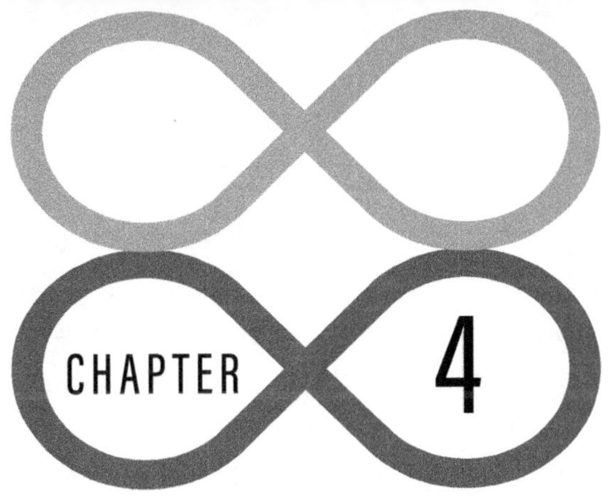

CHAPTER 4

I - IDENTITY

'Being blind to parts of ourselves means that there is often a difference between the person we think we are— or the person we would like to see ourselves as—and who we really are as we walk through the world.'

– Beatrice Chestnut

In order to lead others, you first need to lead yourself. And in order to lead yourself, you need to know yourself, and have a conscious understanding of your strengths and challenges, fears and motivations.

This is identity.

When you don't have a deep understanding of your identity, you're essentially blind to yourself. You aren't self-aware. On the other hand, having an understanding of your identity is what allows you to take off your mask and show up as your authentic self in your life and your leadership.

When I look at the times that I was an excellent leader, they were times when I was operating from a high level of self-awareness. They were the times when I was able to accomplish a lot without becoming overwhelmed. I compare this to the times when I wasn't as self-aware, and it was during these times that I was operating from a place of overwhelm, where I didn't seem to know who I was or operate in alignment with that, and it was then what I feared most, letting people down, became a self-fulling prophecy.

This chapter is focused on the first element of INFINITE Leadership – identity. Why is it first? Because who we are, who we aspire to be, and who we can become is the foundation of becoming an INFINITE Leader.

Your identity isn't set in stone

The first thing to understand is that your identity isn't set in stone. Vusi Thembekwayo once said, 'Identity is man-made, so, therefore, it can be man-changed.' When I heard this for the first time, it literally changed my life. What I realised is that often our identities are made up of so many different things – the stories we tell ourselves and those that are bestowed upon us. We wear a multitude of identities that we give ourselves, like 'sporty' or 'impatient' or identities given to us by other people, even back when we were kids, like 'you're the cheeky kid' or 'you're the class clown', or as adults like 'the single parent' or 'the hothead'. When it comes to identity, we don't really have just one identity – we have many.

But what we often don't recognise is that we have the power to change an identity that maybe doesn't fit with us anymore. That is a mic drop moment. It is powerful. If I don't like something, I have the power to change it! And just like that, you have taken your first step on the path to INFINITE Leadership.

Why finding your identity matters

Before we can determine what parts of our identity are no longer serving us, we have to first determine who we already are. We have to understand what kinds of stories make up our identity for ourselves (these are the stories of our lives), and then see the underlying elements that drive those stories for us. Once we do that, we can change those identities (if we want). But we can't change something we're not aware of.

Understanding your identity – well really, your identities – is like laying the foundation of your house. It's the thing that you build your INFINITE Leadership on. It's the key to understanding the root cause of any challenges you're facing in your leadership journey, personally and professionally.

To drive meaningful change, it's essential to grasp the underlying needs that drive our behaviours. Identity both directly and indirectly influences our behaviour. Each action we take is a response to a fundamental need – one that, if unaddressed, can lead to frustration and stalled progress.

For example, in the case of weight loss surgery, patients often undergo psychological evaluations beforehand, not to dissuade them but to explore their relationship with food. This isn't merely a physical transformation. It's about addressing the emotional roots that contribute to their eating habits. Without understanding these deeper needs, the surgery serves as a temporary fix, rather than a lasting solution. The same concept applies to any behavioural change. If the root need remains unaddressed, even the most sophisticated strategies can fall short, leading to disappointment, disengagement and ultimately feeling like a failure.

In both personal growth and leadership, addressing surface-level issues without exploring underlying motivations often results in disillusionment.

If a leader implements strategies without aligning them to the core needs of their team or themselves, those strategies will likely miss the mark, leading to frustration. It's only by identifying and understanding these needs that we can replace ineffective behaviours with actions that drive genuine progress, fulfilment and lasting change.

Not understanding one's own identity as a leader can be a significant barrier to career advancement, including missing out on promotions. When leaders are unclear about the core values, motivations and needs driving their behaviour, they may struggle to align their actions with the expectations of higher leadership roles. Just as failing to address the root causes of disengagement or turnover in a team leads to ineffective solutions, a leader who lacks self-awareness may implement strategies or adopt leadership styles that don't resonate with their team, peers, or senior leadership. This misalignment can prevent them from demonstrating the qualities required for advancement.

For instance, a leader aiming for a promotion may focus on delivering results but neglect the relational or visionary aspects of leadership. Without understanding that their need for validation or control might be driving their behaviour, they may come across as micromanaging or disconnected from their team. Just as a CEO who doesn't address staff's core needs might struggle with disengagement, a leader who doesn't understand their own identity might fail to build the influence, trust or leadership presence necessary for higher roles. The result? Missed opportunities and the frustration of feeling 'stuck' despite trying various tactics. Gaining clarity on one's leadership identity allows for greater authenticity, strategic alignment, and, ultimately, career progression.

Imposter syndrome

If our identities don't resonate with our true selves we might find ourselves stuck in imposter syndrome.

I think we can all relate to having imposter syndrome, the feeling that we'll be 'found out' or exposed, despite our successes and accomplishments. Seth Godin has a really great quote about imposter syndrome. He says, 'Yes, you're an imposter. But you're an imposter acting in service of generosity, seeking to make things better. When we embrace imposter syndrome instead of working to make it disappear, we choose the productive way forward. The imposter is proof that we're innovating, leading, and creating.'[30]

When we're struggling with imposter syndrome it can feel like getting caught with your pants down. We feel vulnerable and exposed, and it's really about unconscious awareness, or unconscious existing. It's when you're going through life unaware and then find yourself genuinely being surprised when things happen to you.

I had an experience where I was sitting at a Global CEO round table, and we were talking about an important but challenging topic. As the discussion progressed, I have to admit I was sitting wondering, 'What do I have to contribute to this anyway?' But I listened to everybody's stories and perspectives, and at the end, I put up my hand, and made just a couple of key points. After the meeting ended I had so many people come up to me afterward to compliment me on my comments, saying they were so insightful and that they'd never thought about it that way.

If I had gotten in my own way and let my imposter syndrome stop me from putting my hand up, I wouldn't have been able to share and make the connections that I was in a position to make. By doing so I was able

---

30   Godin, S. (2020). *Practice: Shipping Creative*. Portfolio.

to share a bit of insight and help others to be more conscious in their thinking, and that has, hopefully, positively impacted their work moving forward.

Acknowledging our stories

In my work, I've found it's really important to understand that our identity creates how we show up. And if we're unaware of some of the drivers behind how we see our identity, it can unconsciously impact how we show up – and not always in a great way. These are the 'stories' we believe about ourselves.

For example, this might be the workaholic who has unconsciously fed themselves the story that they need to prove themselves. It could be the person who falls in and out of work because their story is that they 'can't cut it'. It could be the person who never speaks up for themselves because they believe it's the only way for them to feel accepted by everybody. It could be the person that actually doesn't go for the promotion unless they are guaranteed to get it. So they hold themselves back because of that need for assurance and lack of inherent self-worth and because they believe they're only as good as the value they bring to the table.

If we want to change our identities, we need to change our stories. But holding space for these stories without judging is also very difficult. It's very easy to get caught in the blame game, or in feeling bad, guilty or ashamed. In spite of this, if we can reach deep and understand what drives our stories without judging, then we're in a position to understand how we unconsciously end up in our patterns. It is then we can make more conscious and informed choices going forward.

Acknowledge how you have grown

Oprah Winfrey has famously said, 'Turn your wounds into wisdom.' And this holds true for the stories that shape our identities. Personally, I have seen so much wisdom come out of my wounds and my experiences and I have also observed that happening for others.

When it comes to changing our identities – at least those that aren't working for us – a big part of this process is about reflecting on the wisdom you've learned. But to do that you first need to acknowledge what happened to you.

That doesn't mean that you should sit in it, bathe in it or dwell on it. However, it is nearly impossible to change something that you don't acknowledge. I think it's really important to notice the distance you've travelled, and acknowledge where you were, where you are, and what and who you're trying to be (an INFINITE Leader!). You might find that yesterday you didn't want to get out of bed, but today, you got out of bed. Sometimes it's as small as that. On other days, you might acknowledge that the old me would have reacted really poorly to a certain situation. But the version of myself that I currently am is choosing to let that go.

There is a Japanese proverb 'Nana korobi ya oki' which translates to 'Fall down seven times, get up eight'. This speaks to the concept of resilience and teaches us that no matter how many times you get knocked down it is important to get back up again. When you're looking at the stories that shape you, don't just focus on the distance travelled, but celebrate the times when you fell down, picked yourself back up and recognised that tomorrow is a new day. Acknowledging where you have grown is so important to have the energy to continue to change.

It can be difficult because often we're so focused on what we're doing poorly that we don't consciously take time to acknowledge what went well. We have to look at the positive growth and not just the adverse experience. So don't allow yourself to just sit and dwell in the negative, but be sure to acknowledge the positive in your journey as well. Again, this comes back to being conscious of who we were, who we are now and who we are aspiring to be, and continuing to evolve our identity to meet our needs.

Gabby Bernstein talks about embracing the opportunity to choose again.[31] So if you're succumbing to negative thoughts, you have the power to choose to shift away from those negative thoughts and choose a different pathway.

Give yourself permission to change your mind (and your identities)

Organisational psychologist Adam Grant talks about the power of thinking again, making the point that you don't have to remain defined by your past.[32] You have the right to use new information you have gained to think in a new way and make a new choice. While the old you may have believed strongly in a particular idea, if you've learned some new information that has allowed you to craft up a new way of thinking, that's actually okay.

You can change your mind.[33]

---

31 Bernstein, G. (2019). *Super Attractor: Methods for Manifesting a Life Beyond Your Wildest Dreams*. Hay House.

32 Shah, V. (19 October 2023). 'A Conversation with Adam Grant on Why We Need to Think Again, About Everything.' Thought Economics. https://thoughteconomics.com/adam-grant/.

33 Shah. A Conversation with Adam Grant on Why We Need to Think Again, About Everything.

In the same way, you don't need to die on the hill of who you have been. You don't have to accept any former version of yourself. We are constantly evolving beings, and we need to acknowledge that in our journey. Something you believed five years ago may no longer serve you and it's okay for you to change your mind.

How to change your identities

If you decide that there are one or more of your identities that need to be changed, now is the time to do that. It will take some work, but is also a hugely valuable part (and the foundation!) of your own INFINITE Leadership journey. And you start by ensuring that your identities align with your values.

Bringing your identities in line with your values

Once we have acknowledged who we have been and the stories that shape us, and we have learned that it's okay to change our minds and revisit how this impacts our identities, we can begin to bring our identity in line with our values as they stand today.

Brené Brown has done a lot of work around how our values guide us and often unconsciously determine our personal leadership trigger points. She says, 'Living into our values means that we do more than profess our values, we practise them.'[34] Practising your values is exactly what INFINITE Leaders do. But it takes digging deep to find those.

I run a lot of workshops, and sometimes I work with parents who have young children with a diagnosis, or who struggle with behaviour. Often these parents are concerned when, in a moment of dysregulation,

---

34   Brown, B. (2018). *Dare to Lead*. Vermilion - Mass Market.

their child breaks something valuable. For a lot of the dads, the act of breaking something is a trigger because they've got a core value set in financial stability. So they might find themselves more triggered than the mum, who's got potentially a different value spectrum and is perhaps more focused on the value of family. But when valuable property gets damaged, dad gets very upset because, whether he recognises it or not, he sees the damage to the property as impacting one of his core values around how he is going to provide for his family.

To be clear, I am not saying dads don't care or don't see family as important, but it has often been ingrained in them that their role is to be the primary provider for the family – particularly those raised in more 'traditional' family structures. And this upbringing creates triggers that impact how they manage certain actions. We have the same types of value drivers in our roles as leaders as well.

One of the real things I recognised in my own life was that integrity was a key value for me and continues to be. How this plays out for me is that, if I feel like my integrity is being called into question, I have to actually take a pause and go back and ask myself, 'Is there truth in the statement? Have I inadvertently done something to let somebody down, or have I not shown up in the way that I wanted to? If so, for what reason?'

If I answer those questions and realise that there is truth to what the other person is saying, then I know I need to repair and course correct that. But if I haven't, then I have to be very careful not to let my personal trigger around my value of integrity get in the way of me being able to show up as the best version of a leader.

One of the key ways to know what your values are is to reflect on what it looks, sounds and feels like when you're walking in alignment, and what it looks, sounds and feels like if you're walking out of alignment. You'll be able to tell when you're walking out of alignment because that's when you have the biggest reactions and feelings (often negative) and these can help you to see what your core values truly are.

Finding these core values is vital to becoming an INFINITE Leader, both so you can align with them and so you can rework the stories that support them if needed. It's also a good idea to find the aspirational values that you would like to build into your life and leadership, and which can help you become more aligned in the future. One of the best ways to find these values is to do the values-based activity below.

Value-Based Model

Abundance	Communication	Excitement
Acceptance	Community	Experience
Accomplishment	Compassion	Expertise
Accountability	Competence	Exploration
Accuracy	Confidence	Fairness
Achievement	Consistency	Faith
Adaptability	Contentment	Fame
Adventure	Contribution	Family
Affection	Control	Fearless
Alertness	Cooperation	Fidelity
Ambition	Courage	Fitness
Assertiveness	Courtesy	Focus
Attentive	Creativity	Foresight
Authenticity	Credibility	Forgiveness
Awareness	Curiosity	Freedom
Balance	Decisiveness	Friendship
Beauty	Dedication	Fun
Boldness	Dependability	Generosity
Bravery	Determination	Giving
Brilliance	Devotion	Goodness
Calmness	Dignity	Grace
Capable	Discipline	Gratitude
Careful	Diversity	Growth
Caring	Efficiency	Happiness
Certainty	Empathy	Hard
Challenge	Endurance	Work
Charity	Energy	Harmony
Cleanliness	Enjoyment	Health
Clear	Enthusiasm	Honesty
Clever	Equality	Honor
Comfort	Ethical	Humility
Commitment	Excellence	Humor
		Imagination

Value-Based Model con't

Independence	Patriotism	Speed
Individuality	Peace	Spirituality
Inner Harmony	Playfulness	Stability
Innovation	Poise	Status
Insightful	Positivity	Stewardship
Inspiring	Power	Strength
Integrity	Productivity	Structure
Intelligence	Professionalism	Success
Intuitive	Prosperity	Support
Joy	Purpose	Surprise
Justice	Quality	Sustainability
Kindness	Recognition	Teamwork
Knowledge	Respect	Temperance
Lawful	Responsibility	Thankful
Leadership	Restraint	Thorough
Learning	Results-oriented	Thoughtful
Logic	Rigor	Timeliness
Love	Security	Tolerance
Loyalty	Self-actualisation	Toughness
Mastery	Self-development	Traditional
Maturity	Self-reliance	Tranquility
Meaning	Self-respect	Transparency
Moderation	Selfless	Trustworthy
Motivation	Sensitivity	Understanding
Obedience	Serenity	Uniqueness
Openness	Service	Unity
Optimism	Sharing	Vision
Order	Silence	Vitality
Organisation	Simplicity	Wealth
Originality	Sincerity	Welcoming
Passion	Skillfulness	Winning
Patience	Solitude	Wisdom

1. Take some time to read through and tick all the values that are important to you.

2. Then go through and halve the list (approximately).

3. Then go through and halve the list again.

4. And then go through and halve the list again. Complete these steps until you get down to two to five values. These are your core values.

5. When you get down to your core values, write each one down and then describe the behaviour that shows up when you are walking in and out of alignment with that value. What do you notice about your reactions? How do you feel?

6. Finally, ask yourself, how do you hold space for people that have different values to you?

This can be a challenging activity because it makes you really dive deeply into what is truly important to you. I would encourage you to take your time, and sit with your thoughts about your values. Don't rush the process. Until you know what values drive you, you aren't going to be in a position to make the changes you need to become a true INFINITE Leader.

Tools for change

I once was engaged to support an executive leadership team where there appeared to be a misalignment around communication preferences and conflict resolution styles, and because of that people weren't getting what they needed. Individuals were feeling really frustrated and the entire leadership team was feeling very disjointed and certainly not operating as a high-performing team. I was able to help the team establish a process involving one-on-one coaching, group coaching and the use of a personality profiling tool. It made a huge difference to how the team functioned, mostly because we chose the right tool for the situation.

When working in this space, I have a particular preference for certain profiling tools. But it's important to pick one that helps create a common language before adding more tools to the mix. This sets the foundation for you to work from.

Choosing the right profiling tool

Over the years, I've explored many different profiling tools. While there are a lot of really great ones, it's important that, no matter what we choose, we don't get trapped into thinking that we are just a number or letter or even a combination of letters. The tool's results are there to provide you with insight about your identity – not to define your entire identity.

When it comes to understanding my own leadership identity, the tool that I consider the foundation of my own INFINITE Leadership is the Enneagram.

The Enneagram

There is a tagline on an Enneagram Instagram page that says, 'If the Enneagram is not hurting your feelings a little bit you're probably not doing it right'. This really resonated with me because this was the first profiling tool that really challenged me and gave me a pathway to a healthier, more aligned version of myself. While some other tools that I've worked through have given me a spotlight on who I am, and talked about my positives and my negatives, the Enneagram framed it as the 'healthy' and 'unhealthy' version of myself, which really helped me to make the changes that I needed for myself.

With the healthy and unhealthy versions, I could then visualise this pathway running between them (and back again). This gave me a map of what I needed to do if I started to notice myself straying into an unhealthy version of myself. It gave me the ability to turn back down the path toward a more healthy version of myself and, in turn, that has meant that I haven't found myself heading toward unhealth as frequently or for as long a period of time.

The Enneagram explained

The Enneagram is described as a '3 x 3 arrangement of nine personality types in three 'Centers'. There are three types in the Instinctive Center, three in the Feeling Center, and three in the Thinking Center…. Each Center consists of three personality types that have in common the assets and liabilities of that Center. For example, personality type Four has unique strengths and liabilities involving its feelings, which is why it is in the Feeling Center. Likewise, the Eight's assets and liabilities involve its relationship to its instinctual drives, which is why it is in the Instinctive Center, and so forth for all nine personality types.'[35]

---

35   (2024). 'How the Enneagram System Works.' The Enneagram Institute.
       https://www.enneagraminstitute.com/how-the-enneagram-system-
       works/#:~:text=The%20Enneagram%20is%20a%203,and%20liabilities%20of%20
       that%20Center.

Of the nine different types of personalities, you will have one basic personality type. But rather than showing this as static, The Enneagram contemplates that you will fluctuate constantly among the healthy and unhealthy traits that make up your personality type (including both your superpowers and your kryptonite).[36]

What's imperative to understand is that with the Enneagram no personality type is inherently better or worse than any other. All have unique assets and unique challenges. However, what you can take away from this is that, when you understand your core personality type, you're able to leverage this to become your best version of yourself both personally and professionally.[37]

---

36   How the Enneagram System Works.
37   How the Enneagram System Works.

I – Identity

ENNEAGRAM	BURNING QUESTION	SUPERPOWERS	YES	KRYPTONITE	NO
1 Reformer	Am I in integrity?	Systems improvement / Consistent excellence	I feel virtous and good	Making mistakes / Lack of accountability	I feel defective / corrupt, bad
2 Helper	Am I loved?	Community-building / service	I feel cared for and worthy of love	Rejection, cricitism / Lack of community	I feel rejected, unloved, unwanted
3 Motivator	Am I worthy and accepted?	Goal & results-driven / Public face	I feel valued and succesful	Failure, losing face / No room to shine	I feel worthless like a failure
4 Artist	Am I unique?	Creativity, insight / Emotional intelligence	I feel special and seen	Superficiality / Cog in the machine	I feel invisible and unimportant
5 Thinker	Am I capable and competent?	Innovative, pioneering / Highly competent	I feel masterful and like an expert	Risk-taking / Improvised performance	I feel useless and incapable
6 Loyalist	Am I secure and supported?	Healthy skepticism / Team cohesion/stability	I feel safe and grounded	Risk, instability / Lack of support	I feel neglected and abandoned
7 Enthusiast	Am I satisfied and happy?	Prolific, visionary / Positive energy	I feel free, joyful full of life	Routine, confinement / Micro-management	I feel trapped and deprived
8 Challenger	Am I safe and in control?	Heroic leadership / Direct resolution	I feel strong and powerful	Indirect communication / Inefficiency, injustice	I feel vulnerable and violated
9 Peacemaker	Am I at peace?	Grounded leadership / Mediation	I feel connected and harmonious	Conflict, disconnection / Self-assertion	I feel alon and ungrounded

Other profiling tools

Many people are familiar with tools like Myers-Briggs, DISC, Strengths and other similar tools. Each can provide valuable information, especially in the leadership context. And some may provide better insights at different times, particularly when your work environment changes. My suggestion is to investigate the different profiling tools, to find out what gives you the best understanding of where you are and a pathway to get where you want to be.

Myers-Briggs

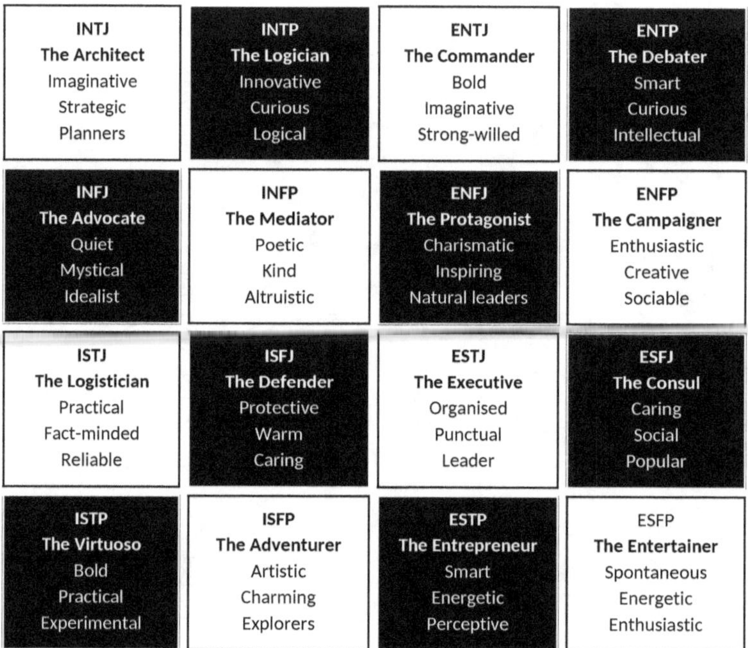

The Myers-Briggs Type Indicator (MBTI) is a personality profiling tool designed to help people better understand themselves and others by identifying their preferences in how they perceive the world and make decisions. Based on Carl Jung's theories, it categorises individuals into one of 16 personality types, using four overarching themes: Extraversion vs. Introversion, Sensing vs. Intuition, Thinking vs. Feeling and Judging vs. Perceiving. This tool is often used to improve communication, enhance teamwork and foster personal development. When used with integrity, it can help leaders and teams build stronger, more understanding work environments.

DiSC

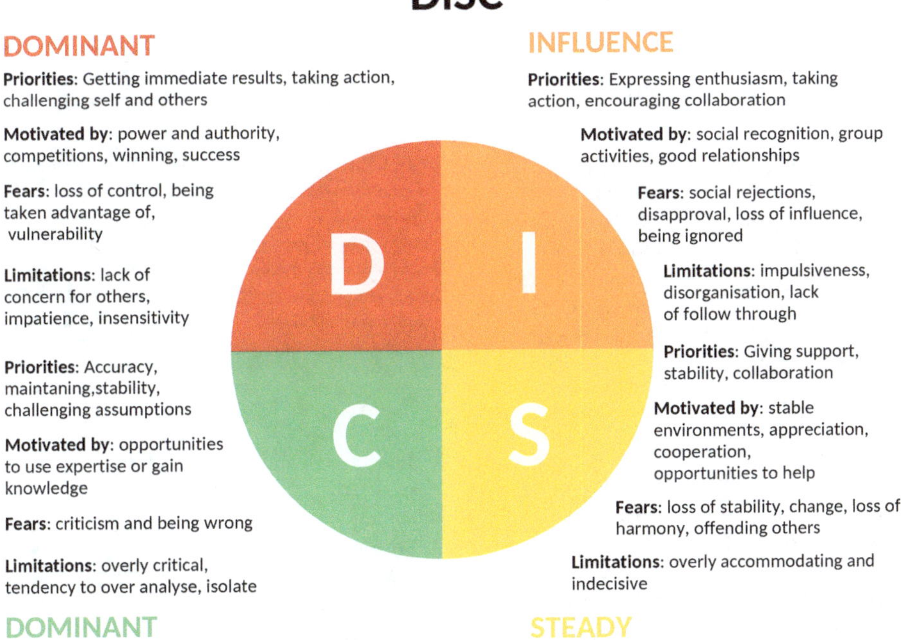

The DiSC personality profiling tool is a widely used behavioural assessment designed to help individuals understand their own communication and work styles, as well as those of others. DiSC categorises behaviour into four primary dimensions: Dominance (D), Influence (I), Steadiness (S) and Conscientiousness (C). Each dimension reflects different preferences for decision-making, communication and interactions with others. The tool is commonly applied in workplace settings to enhance teamwork, communication and leadership effectiveness by fostering greater self-awareness and improving how individuals relate to colleagues with differing styles.

Unlike some personality assessments, DiSC focuses on observable behaviours rather than deep psychological traits, making it highly practical for immediate application in team dynamics and leadership contexts.

Clifton Strengths Assessment

EXECUTING	INFLUENCING	RELATIONSHIP BUILDING	STRATEGIC THINKING
People with dominant executing themes know how to make things happen.	People with dominant influencing themes know how to take charge, speak up, and make sure the team is heard.	People with dominant relationship building themes have the ability to build strong relationships that can hold a team together and make the team greater than the sum of its parts.	People with dominant strategic thinking themes help teams consider what could be. They absorb and analyse information that can inform better decisions.
Achiever Arranger Belief Consistency Deliberative Discipline Focus Responsibility Restorative	Activator Command Communication Competition Self-assurance Maximiser Significance Woo	Adaptability Connectedness Developer Empathy Harmony Includer Individualisation Positivity Relator	Analytical Context Futuristic Ideation Input Intellection Learner Strategic

There has been a profound shift in the last few years to focusing on and leveraging our strengths rather than constantly aiming to improve our weaknesses. Don Clifton was ahead of the game when he pioneered his approach in 1949. In his work he focused on the key question, 'What would happen if we studied what was *right* with people versus what's wrong with people?'.[38]

We tend to be so focused on our deficits due to what is known as the negativity bias. This is our tendency as humans to register and dwell more readily on negative stimuli.[39] But it's equally important to recognise our strengths.

Research tells us that it takes five positives to negate any negative.[40] So while we should make note of what's not working well, it's also equally important to look at our strengths and not let our positives be overwhelmed by our negatives.

There's more and more evidence coming out showing that when we work from a strengths-based framework, we're better able to find ourselves and where we fit as a part of our team, as well as finding people for our teams that are complementary to our own strengths, rather than just not employing in our likeness.[41] This allows us to create a diverse team that has a multitude of strengths to get the best outcome. That is INFINITE Leadership.

When you're looking at your identity as a leader, it's also really important to look at your strengths and how they show up in your role. The Clifton Strengths Assessment is a great way to do that.

---

38 (2024). 'The History of CliftonStrengths.' Gallup. https://www.gallup.com/cliftonstrengths/en/253754/history-cliftonstrengths.aspx.

39 Cherry, K. (13 November 2023). 'What Is the Negativity Bias?' Verywell Mind. https://www.verywellmind.com/negative-bias-4589618.

40 Benson, K. (18 September 2024). 'The Magic Relationship Ratio, According to Science.' The Gottman Institute. https://www.gottman.com/blog/the-magic-relationship-ratio-according-science/.

41 Miglianico, M et al. (1 March 2019). 'Strength Use in the Workplace: A Literature Review.' *Journal of Happiness Studies.* https://doi.org/10.1007/s10902-019-00095-w.

The Clifton Strengths has four 4 overarching categories:

1. **Executing** – Making things happen.

2. **Influencing** – Speaking up, ensuring the team is heard and taking charge.

3. **Relationship Building** – Making the team greater as a whole, and holding it together.

4. **Strategic thinking** – Absorbing and analysing information to make better decisions.

Within these overarching categories, there are 34 specific strengths. While individual people tend to have a dominant category, many combinations exist. Like with personality type tools, no one set of strengths is greater than the other. But their benefit is in the insights they provide. Instead it's important to understand how these can impact your leadership thinking and action-taking. The best teams have a diverse cross-section of people and also have the skills to create strong psychological safety and establish high levels of trust and communication (which we'll explore in later chapters).

Understanding strengths is a vital part of INFINITE Leadership and personal identity development because it helps leaders and employees align their natural talents with their work. Leaders who focus on strengths not only engage employees more effectively but also create an environment where individuals feel valued and motivated. This approach enhances both individual and team performance, leading to higher productivity, lower turnover and stronger organisational outcomes. When leaders encourage strengths, they foster a deeper connection between people and their roles, supporting sustainable success.

Putting theory into practice

It's vital to understand that profiling tools simply give us information. INFINITE Leadership is about what we do with that information. Tools only work when you can apply them in context and use them to become consciously aware of your unconscious patterns.

A very good friend and colleague of mine told me his boss used the 'Surrounded by Idiots' framework by Thomas Erickson, which categorises personalities into colours, red, yellow, blue, and green types. During a conversation, my friend's boss referred to him as a 'red'. I paused and decided I needed to explore further. I went and did some research on the specific tool, and the next time I caught up with him I asked him an important question around identity. I asked, 'Do you identify as a red, or does your work environment require you to be a red for the role you're navigating?' He identified that he saw himself more as a yellow. I explained that I experienced him much more as a 'yellow', with a tinge of 'red'.

This reflection was pivotal for him because, despite loving his job, he was beginning to feel burnt out and overwhelmed at the time, having to take on a role that didn't align with his natural zone of genius but that he was doing because he was exceptionally competent at it.

This understanding gave him real insights into his working life and he realised that he needed to move out of the red for his wellbeing. Since then he's been able to have the conversation with his boss and explain what he needed in order to live more aligned with his authentic self. He explained that he was given this role because the organisation was going through significant change and they needed someone to drive the ship who could be quite directive, which he was very capable of doing. But he now understood that if he stayed in that purely red space for too long he would continue to feel fatigued and that could lead to a feeling of resentment.

My friend's story is not unique. I am sure all of us at some time have been put in a position of misalignment. The challenge is how to move towards healthier alignment which will always lead to greater success.

This real-life experience shows that while tools can provide insights, they shouldn't define us entirely. There are many factors to consider, and the environment can play a huge role.

At the end of the day, none of the profiling tools define who you are. They can, however, give you insight into how to develop your best leadership capabilities – these are your INFINITE Leadership capabilities.

From awareness to transformation

When we are going through the process of exploring our identities on the path to INFINITE Leadership, we can begin to see behind the masks we wear. And let's be honest, we all wear masks as leaders. These masks might be who we think we need to be in a role, or who we believe we actually are. We're often trying to hide behind these masks in an attempt to put our best foot forward.

The most important piece of advice I can give during this identity journey is to be kind to yourself. Recognise that the version of yourself in the past did what it needed to do in order to maintain a sense of safety. So continue to be kind to your past self. This journey is about moving towards the healthier version of ourselves so that we can truly become INFINITE Leaders. Sometimes this involves engaging somebody from the outside – like a coach – to hold space for the brave and courageous conversations that we might struggle to have on our own.

INFINITE Leadership is about applying the insights you learn from self-reflection and tools and putting those insights into everyday practice. It's about leading ourselves so we can lead both ourselves and others effectively and evolve into the best version of ourselves as leaders. By becoming aware of our stories and patterns, we consciously choose who we want to be, rather than letting our unconscious stories and habits define us.

There's a saying that's been around for years that says, 'It didn't happen to you; it happened for you.' I've been through enough awful experiences in my life, and I have witnessed others going through similar, so much so that I couldn't ever seem to reconcile that statement. I've lived through my own experience with domestic violence. I had a friend who, with her children, was stabbed multiple times. I've had another friend navigate chemotherapy when her child was still too young to understand what was happening. I've also been bullied for being a single mum.

All of these horrible situations make it hard to reconcile that statement – how can these things happen 'for' us? However, if we can find the wisdom from these wounds, it makes it slighty easier to move forward.

While it may not always seem reconcilable with difficult experiences, understanding how these moments shape us allows us to move forward and grow. Not in a bitter or defeatist way, but by acknowledging that we are the sum of our experiences, which is what makes us unique. We can use this lens to gain a new perspective on the world, which then allows us to input and value add into the world.

By harnessing our tools, developing self-awareness and exercising self-compassion, we can take intentional steps towards creating positive changes in our lives and identities and, ultimately, in our leadership, whether your focus is on your personal or professional journey.

 ## Reflection Questions

To find your own INFINITE identity pillar ask yourself these questions for reflection:

1. What is the story you tell yourself about yourself as a person, and as a leader?

2. Is the identity you currently have one that you have consciously created or one that you have accumulated? Who do you aspire to be?

3. What do you need to let go of to be the leader that you want to be, both personally and professionally?

4. How can you ensure your leadership identity continues to evolve in a way that reflects both your personal growth and the needs of the people and organisations you lead?

As we continue on this journey of self-discovery and growth that will take us into the space of INFINITE Leadership, the next step is to delve into the importance of nurture – nurturing our emotional intelligence, trust and mindset – the foundation upon which we build deeper connections and cultivate resilience.

'Becoming a leader is synonymous with becoming yourself. It is precisely that simple, and it is also that difficult.'

– Warren Bennis

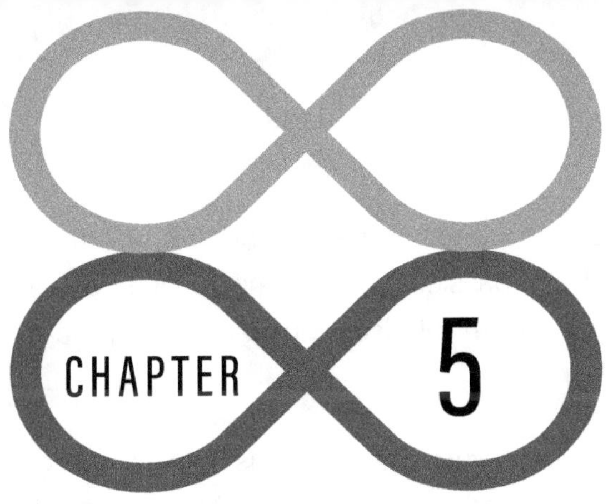

N - NURTURE

'Leaders who nurture people are not only helping individuals grow but are also creating a culture of continuous improvement and loyalty within their teams.'
– John C Maxwell

The second pillar of the INFINITE Leadership model is nurture. And like John Maxwell's quote teaches us, nurturing is not just about the people – it's also about the overall culture in our teams and organisations. That includes and begins with nurturing yourself.

Why nurture matters in INFINITE Leadership

Nurture is a crucial pillar on the path to becoming an INFINITE Leader. That's because true leadership – INFINITE Leadership – goes beyond managing tasks or managing people. It requires cultivating a supportive environment where individuals feel valued and empowered.

To begin to nurture our teams, we also need to nurture ourselves. This begins with self-compassion and then moves on to building trust within teams, fostering growth mindsets and embracing ideals of emotional intelligence.

An INFINITE Leader knows that a team is only as strong as its ability to navigate challenges and adapt to change. This adaptability comes from nurturing emotional intelligence – understanding our own emotions and those of others and responding with empathy and agility. When we're able to nurture relationships and foster trust, we lay the groundwork for open communication, innovation and collaboration. Nurture transforms the workplace into a place where individuals can thrive and contribute their best selves, and it's a hallmark of a strong, empathetic and INFINITE leader.

Over the course of this chapter, we'll delve into the components of this nurture pillar, including competency, self-compassion, trust, mindset, emotional intelligence, insight and agility, and how each of these can help us move along our journey into INFINITE Leadership. But first, we need to start with what might hold us back.

Barriers to nurture

There are five key challenges leaders may face personally and professionally as they work to develop the nurturing skills necessary for INFINITE Leadership:

	Personally	Professionally
1	Self-Judgement: People may have unrelenting standards, Through internal and external reinforcement, self-compassion may not have been something they have been exposed to, or taught. Perfectionism is a defensive move with the goal of gaining approval and acceptance, which in turn undermines resilience. It halts our growth and stops us from being authentically seen and known.	Perfectionism and Self-Criticism: Leaders often hold themselves to unrealistic standards, which makes it hard to embrace self-compassion. Perfectionism creates a cycle of self-judgement that stalls personal growth and undermines resilience. Without breaking this cycle, it becomes difficult for leaders to fully engage and grow.
2	Lack of Safe Spaces: We all want to feel seen, heard, loved and accepted. When we don't feel that we are, it stops us from challenging our own thoughts as well as those of others.	Lack of Psychological Safety: To build trust within a team or organisation, leaders need to create an environment where people feel safe taking risks. Without psychological safety, team members are less likely to be open, and the leader's ability to nurture innovation and collaboration is compromised.
3	Fixed Mindset: Being rigid and closed-minded in our thinking stops us from seeing opportunities and possibilities.	Fixed Mindset: Adopting a growth mindset is essential but challenging when leaders feel pressured to always prove their competence. A fixed mindset leads to avoiding challenges, which limits both personal development and the ability to empower others to grow.
4	Emotional Blind Spots: Understanding and acknowledging that we each have triggers and parts of ourselves that are harder to see.	Emotional Blind Spots: Emotional intelligence is critical to effective leadership, but many leaders face challenges in identifying their own emotional triggers and understanding the emotions of others. When leaders are unaware of their emotional blind spots, it becomes difficult to create the trust and empathy needed to build strong teams.
5	Resistance to Change: Stops us from showing up and doing the work to get to the outcome and the connections we truly want.	Resistance to Change: Developing agility requires an openness to change, but many leaders resist new ideas or approaches, fearing that change will disrupt their control or comfort. Without agility, leaders struggle to adapt to evolving challenges, and this lack of flexibility can limit their effectiveness in nurturing both themselves and others.

We're also held back by our lack of competence

It's important to also touch on the idea of competence, which is something that can hold us back from becoming nurturers, but that lies outside of the framework above. How does competence hold us back? Well, it's because competence is something you acquire rather than something you innately have, yet we're all expected to simply *be competent* when we become leaders. But without being taught how to be a leader, how can we become a competent leader –an INFINITE Leader?

Unconscious Incompetence

"You don't know what you don't know"

Unconscious Competence

"Second Nature"

Conscious Incompetence

"You know what you don't know"

Conscious Competence

"You know what you know"

Noel Burch's Four Stages of Competence is a widely recognised framework that describes the progression individuals go through when learning new skills. And let's be honest, learning to truly nurture ourselves and others is not something many of us have been taught, and certainly not mastered, yet it is foundational to our fulfilment and development as individuals, teams and organisations.

These stages are:

1. Unconscious incompetence
2. Conscious incompetence
3. Conscious competence
4. Unconscious competence

Understanding this model is essential both as individuals and in the context of leadership because it helps us identify where we and our teams are in the learning process, allowing everyone to provide the right kind of support and nurturing.

In the first stage, unconscious incompetence, individuals are unaware of the skills or knowledge they lack. Leaders at this stage might not realise their deficiencies in critical areas like emotional intelligence or fostering trust. American psychologist Daniel Goleman's work on emotional intelligence points out that self-awareness is the foundation of strong leadership,[42] yet many leaders remain unaware of how their emotions impact their teams.

Recognising this stage allows leaders to create environments where feedback is welcomed and blind spots are uncovered, paving the way for growth. Have you ever had someone really upset you, and be completely blind to the impact they've had? Or the team member who thinks they are doing a stellar job when, in fact, people (most likely you) have to go back in and redo their work, to get it up to scratch. They're often in a bubble, and you're likely flabbergasted at how they don't see it.

---

42 Goleman, D. (2006). Emotional Intelligence: Why It Can Matter More Than IQ. Bantam.

The second stage, conscious incompetence, occurs when individuals become aware of their skills gaps. While this stage can feel uncomfortable, it is critical in nurturing growth. Brené Brown's research on vulnerability emphasises that this stage requires courage, as leaders must confront their imperfections and limitations.[43]

Embracing conscious incompetence allows leaders to model vulnerability, showing their teams that it's okay to not have all the answers. This, in turn, fosters a culture of learning and psychological safety.[44] As a high achiever (which if you are reading this book, you no doubt are) this is probably one of the toughest stages. It can be difficult to sit in the uncomfortableness of being aware you are not as competent as you want or need to be.

Recently I was holding space for a client, who despite being highly intelligent and understanding the theory of what she needed to do, was unable to implement these skills into practice as frequently as she wanted, which caused tension in her leadership. She needed to embrace vulnerability in order to embrace growth.

In the third stage, conscious competence, individuals can perform a task or apply a skill, but they must do so with full attention and effort. This is where mindset and agility come into play. Susan David's work on emotional agility emphasises that leaders must stay flexible and aware of their emotional triggers to effectively manage their teams.[45] At this stage, leaders begin to consciously apply new skills, such as active listening or emotional regulation, but it requires deliberate effort. Encouraging leaders to persevere through this stage helps build resilience and prepares them for the final level. For many this stage is

---

43 Brown, B. (2018). *Dare to Lead*. Vermilion - Mass Market.
44 Sandberg, S & Grant, A. (7 May 2019). *Option B: Facing Adversity, Building Resilience, and Finding Joy.'* WH Allen.
45 David, S. (2017). *Emotional Agility: Get Unstuck, Embrace Change and Thrive in Work and Life*. Penguin (General UK).

fatiguing and frustrating because your brain is ready for the next stage, but your competence and skill muscles (literally and metaphorically) are playing catch-up.

The last stage, unconscious competence, is when a skill becomes second nature. Leaders who reach this stage can intuitively navigate complex emotional and interpersonal dynamics. However, Simon Sinek warns that this stage can also lead to complacency if leaders stop seeking continuous improvement.[46] This is where the concept of INFINITE Leadership comes in – nurturing leaders must continually evolve, staying aware of new challenges and opportunities for growth, even when they've mastered certain skills.

How to build our nurturing capabilities

Now that we understand the things that might stop us from embracing nurture in our leadership, we need to move on to how to do better. And it starts with self-compassion.

Embracing self-compassion

In the context of nurturing, understanding the Four Stages of Competence helps leaders create a supportive learning environment for themselves and their teams. By recognising which stage they or their team members are in, leaders can offer the right balance of challenge and support. As Kristen Neff, a world-leading researcher on compassion and founder of the Mindful Self-Compassion program, explains, self-compassion is essential in this journey. Without it, leaders

---

46   Sinek, S. (2011). *Start with Why: How Great Leaders Inspire Everyone to Take Action.* Sinek, Simon.

might get stuck in the discomfort of conscious incompetence or feel overwhelmed by the effort required in conscious competence.[47]

By fostering patience, empathy, and resilience through these stages, leaders can create a culture that not only nurtures growth but also prepares everyone for the continuous journey of learning and improvement essential to INFINITE Leadership. In our situation, this is where you know you are an INFINITE Leader. One of the key parts in developing our nurture pillar in INFINITE Leadership is self-compassion. But embracing self-compassion is often very, very difficult. Being kind to ourselves during difficult times is not something that we do very well.

I often ask people if the way that they're speaking to themselves is how they would speak to a friend. Of course they say, 'Oh, no, don't be ridiculous. Of course, I wouldn't.' So then I ask, 'How would you talk to yourself if you saw yourself as a friend instead? How could that look different?'

Kristin Neff says, 'Treat yourself with the same kindness you would treat a friend.'[48] She talks about how so many expert psychologists are turning away from a focus on self-esteem and turning towards a focus on self-compassion. The research shows that this focus enables you to achieve your highest potential, but also live a more fulfilled life as well.[49]

Dr Tasha Eurich, who is an organisational psychologist and researcher, also talks about how the key part of self-reflection is having insight into what's going on without judgement.[50] She says that rather than

---

47   Neff, K. (2011). *Self-Compassion: The Proven Power of Being Kind to Yourself.* William Morrow.

48   Neff, K. (2011). *Self-Compassion: The Proven Power of Being Kind to Yourself.* William Morrow.

49   Neff. *Self-Compassion.*

50   Rucker, M. (23 June 2021). 'Interview with Tasha Eurich about Personal Insight.' Michael Rucker. https://michaelrucker.com/thought-leader-interviews/tasha-eurich-personal-insight/.

asking questions like, 'Why am I the way I am?' or, 'Why didn't I get that promotion?' we might say, 'What aspects of my behaviour impacted that outcome?' or, 'What can I learn from this experience of not getting this promotion that will help me in the future?' This is self-reflection, but it's self-reflection with compassion.

Remember Gabby Bernstein's idea that we can choose again? If you don't like a decision or reaction you've had, rather than berating and judging yourself, remember that you have the power to revisit it. We often feel that we must 'die on the hill' of our previous choices out of pride or fear. But we don't need to do that.

I often talk to my clients about having an audit process where we're constantly checking in without judgement. Ask yourself, 'How am I feeling right now? What am I thinking right now? What action or inaction am I taking?' If you can check in without judgement you can avoid being hijacked by your emotions at the expense of being able to make change. It's one of the key things that I see time and time again, whether people are five, 15 or 50 years old.

Developing self-compassion is a vital part of the nurturing pillar. It allows us to move through moments of high emotions a lot more effectively and to engage in nurturing others on our team as well. And once you have compassion for yourself then you're in a better space to start building trust with your team, because you'll be more willing to share your own stories without judgement.

Building trust – the marble jar

Brené Brown gives us a fantastic metaphor for building trust with her marble jar analogy.[51] In this analogy, she talks about how, in order to build trust, we must continually add marbles to the other person's jar through sharing stories about ourselves. The more stories we share, and the deeper these stories are, the more marbles you've added to the jar.

This metaphor shows that trust is a mutual investment. When the time comes that we need the other person to trust us, we can then draw from that jar. But we can only do that if we've been consistently depositing trust marbles in their jar along the way. We can't just expect to be given trust in the first instance – it must be built over time.

I vividly remember a new staff member coming back so frustrated from a meeting with his team leader. He slammed his folders on the table and explained about how he had this great idea, but his leader didn't listen and was dismissive. After validating his idea, I curiously asked him how the idea helped the leader meet his KPIs and secondly, what have you done to earn his trust? In all honesty, he doesn't even know you. Why would he trust your ideas?

He paused and looked at me. The response he received had nothing to do with the quality of his idea, but was instead rooted in the lack of a mutual and reciprocal relationship. While there is no guarantee you'll get what you want, having marbles in the marble jar increases the likelihood of being heard and being able to get your idea off the ground.

Trust is mentioned frequently, but what does it mean? Charles Feltman, a leadership development expert, defines trust as 'choosing to risk

---

51   Brown, B. (1 February 2016). *Daring Greatly: How the Courage to Be Vulnerable Transforms the Way We Live, Love, Parent and Lead.* Penguin Life.

making something you value vulnerable to another person's actions.'[52] He says that trust requires four things – sincerity, reliability, competence and care.

So how do we show up as trusting for others? How do we know that people will trust us? Trust can look different for everybody. It can be remembering your birthday. It can be being discreet. It can be being sincere in our communication or showing care some other way. But when we break trust it's akin to smashing that marble jar and unfortunately it doesn't take much to take away all of the good work that we do. Trust takes time to build, but it only takes a split second to break. I'm sure we've all got examples of people that have broken our trust, and, if we're truly being honest, where we have been less than trustworthy at some stage in our journey. The trick for an INFINITE Leader is learning and taking action from those lessons.

Trust is a cornerstone of nurturing. It's through trust that we create an environment where members feel safe to express themselves, take risks, innovate and openly communicate with you, on a personal level and as a leader. For INFINITE Leadership, nurturing trust means fostering genuine connections and showing that we value others' contributions even when they don't align completely with our ideas. It also means being vulnerable enough to share ourselves with our team. When trust is nurtured it allows for honest communication and collaboration and forms the foundation of a resilient and high-functioning team.

The value of having a growth mindset

'Hope is not a strategy, but without hope, there is no strategy.'

---

52 Feltman, C. (2024). *The Thin Book of Trust: An Essential Primer for Building Trust at Work*. Berrett-Koehler Publishers.

I remember working with a young person who'd been written off by the education system. He was pretty angry with the world and he'd broken his mum's nose twice by the time he was 13. When he came into my world, he was angry at everybody and everything, placing blame on anybody other than himself. He saw no hope for his future beyond school. However, over time, by developing trust, providing him with skills and showing him the possibilities for his life, and by giving him hope about what was possible and what opportunities were out there, we changed the trajectory of his life. He went from being constantly in trouble to earning an early acceptance to university and even receiving a scholarship offer.

Today he continues to thrive. He's added to his certificates, is exploring the idea of volunteering with the fire brigade and is actively pursuing future pathways. This young man had an alphabet soup of diagnoses, and people repeatedly told him what he couldn't do. But by giving him hope he learned that, despite his past and despite his diagnoses, with the right support he could achieve great things. And this changed the trajectory of his life.

A huge part of this young man's transformation was helping him develop a growth mindset. Carol Dweck's work around growth mindset is an imperative part of becoming an INFINITE Leader because when you have a growth mindset you believe that your abilities can be developed. When you have a fixed mindset you believe that the way you are now is how you're going to stay.[53] But nurturing yourself and your team absolutely requires this growth mindset. It's a bit like the concept of kaizen which requires you to continuously review and improve your

---

53   Armstrong, K. (29 October 2019). 'Carol Dweck on How Growth Mindsets Can Bear Fruit in the Classroom.' Association for Psychological Science. https://www. psychologicalscience.org/observer/dweck-growth-mindsets.

processes and actions.[54] But you can't have a growth mindset if you believe that improvement is not possible, and if you don't accept that continuous improvement is a part of our own self development, then you're going to be limiting yourself.

As Henry Ford said, 'Whether you think you can, or you think you can't, you're right.'

Growth mindset is how we 'think we can'. It gives us some light at the end of the tunnel. We need those lights to guide our pathways. Otherwise, what point is there? Often through our own experiences, we can fall into the trap of feeling like we have to be our own light and that we have to do it ourselves. But who are your safe people to hold space for your thoughts? If you can find that safe person – like a coach as we touched on earlier – then you have someone else who can be a guiding light and help you to have a growth mindset.

Tasha Eurich talks about 'loving critics' as opposed to 'unloving critics'.[55] Loving critics help us find a way to focus on opportunities, and when you are able to do this for others through nurturing them, then you're able to help them develop a growth mindset that embraces learning that can lead to growth.

I often joke that we must find the 'unicorn in the pile of poo'. There's a story of an optimistic child who was really, really positive no matter what he got. And so when given a pile of dung eagerly sifted through it saying, 'There has to be a unicorn in here somewhere!'

So what's the lesson? What's the wisdom in the wound? What's the takeaway? What's the learning that can happen? This analogy encourages us to reflect on our experiences and seek out the places

---

54   'What is Kaizen? Dive into the Kaizen methodology.' Kaizen Institute. https://kaizen.com/what-is-kaizen/.

55   Rucker, M. Interview with Tasha Eurich about Personal Insight.

for growth – the learnings or wisdom – that help us distinguish between having a growth mindset and a fixed mindset. And when we can encourage growth mindsets for ourselves and for those we lead, we're in a much stronger position to be a nurturer and we can move further along the pathway to INFINITE Leadership.

Cultivating emotional intelligence

Emotional intelligence (EQ) has had a long day in the sun. But it's not always very well understood. Emotional intelligence is the ability to understand and manage your emotions, as well as recognise and influence the emotions of those around you.[56] It's important to our nurture pillar because it's what helps you successfully lead teams, manage stress, deliver feedback and collaborate.[57] While this has been talked about for years, the gap is in its application, particularly when things are really tough.

Daniel Goleman, who we mentioned earlier in this chapter, is the godfather of emotional intelligence. His work sets out the four pillars of emotional intelligence, which includes self-awareness, self-management, social awareness and social or relational management.[58]

Organisational anthropologist Timothy Clark, well known for his work on psychological safety, expands on Goleman's theories on emotional intelligence by adding two more pillars of emotional intelligence – self-regard and social regard.[59] According to Clark, poor self-regard affects

---

56   Landry, L. (3 April 2019). 'Why emotional intelligence is important in leadership.' Harvard Business School Online. https://online.hbs.edu/blog/post/emotional-intelligence-in-leadership.

57   Landry. Why emotional intelligence is important in leadership.

58   Goleman, D. (2006). Emotional Intelligence: Why It Can Matter More Than IQ. Bantam.

59   (27 September 2024). EQindex™ Field Guide. LeaderFactor. https://www.leaderfactor.com/resources/eqindex-field-guide.

what we take notice of, what we become aware of, and, ultimately, what we manage. Improving our self-regard enhances our ability to achieve better self-awareness, but self-awareness without judgement.

Similarly, social regard shapes how we interact with others. If you go into a meeting with the feeling that your team is lazy or that they're going to let you down, does it influence how you show up in that meeting? On the other hand, if you believe your team is well equipped to handle any challenge that comes their way, you become more socially aware of your team's strengths, and you can manage your team accordingly. That's the benefit of emotional intelligence.

So where do you feel that you sit on the framework of competence around emotional intelligence? Is this something that you do well or execute naturally, without a lot of conscious effort? Or is it something that you have to put an effort into? What happens when you're tired, overwhelmed or dysregulated? How does that impact how you show up into these conversations? How does it affect how you show up with your team? The answer to these questions will help you gather insight into where you are with regard to your ability to nurture yourself and your team on the pathway to INFINITE Leadership.

Emotional intelligence helps you embrace emotional agility

As we now know, in order to navigate our rapidly changing world and become INFINITE Leaders, we need to be able to agilely adapt to our situations. And we need to empower our teams to do the same. Emotional intelligence helps us embrace emotional agility, and so we're better prepared to respond despite challenging situations.

In her book *Emotional Agility*, Susan David talks about the fact that first we need to be aware of our feelings and emotions, and then we need to come up with a new solution that will allow us to be agile and pivot to a new option.[60] David believes that it's vital for us to shake the judgemental opinions of our inner voice so that we can learn to face our emotions with acceptance and generosity and act according to our deepest values.[61] This is certainly part of the INFINITE Leadership nurturing pillar as well because it means that we can understand what's driving our decisions, and when we learn new information, we're able to make a new decision. We don't have to die on the hill.

David defines emotional agility as the ability to be in tune with your emotions, thoughts and experiences without getting bogged down by them.[62] It's about being flexible with your thoughts and feelings so you can respond optimally to different situations. One of the things that I really love about this concept is the fact that we can dig ourselves out of what we're feeling in any particular moment, because our thoughts guide our feelings, our feelings guide our actions or inactions, and these then guide our results, whether they be positive or negative.

Identifying your emotions

David talks about how, in order to respond with emotional agility, we first need to accurately label our emotions.[63] I don't know how many times I've had people come up to me and preface a conversation by saying, 'I'm not angry', when it seems very clear by how they are acting that they are. We need to be able to label our emotions accurately.

If you're not sure how to do that, have a look at my emotions wheel.

---

60   David, S. (2017). *Emotional Agility: Get Unstuck, Embrace Change and Thrive in Work and Life*. Penguin (General UK).

61   David. Emotional Agility.

62   David. Emotional Agility.

63   David. Emotional Agility.

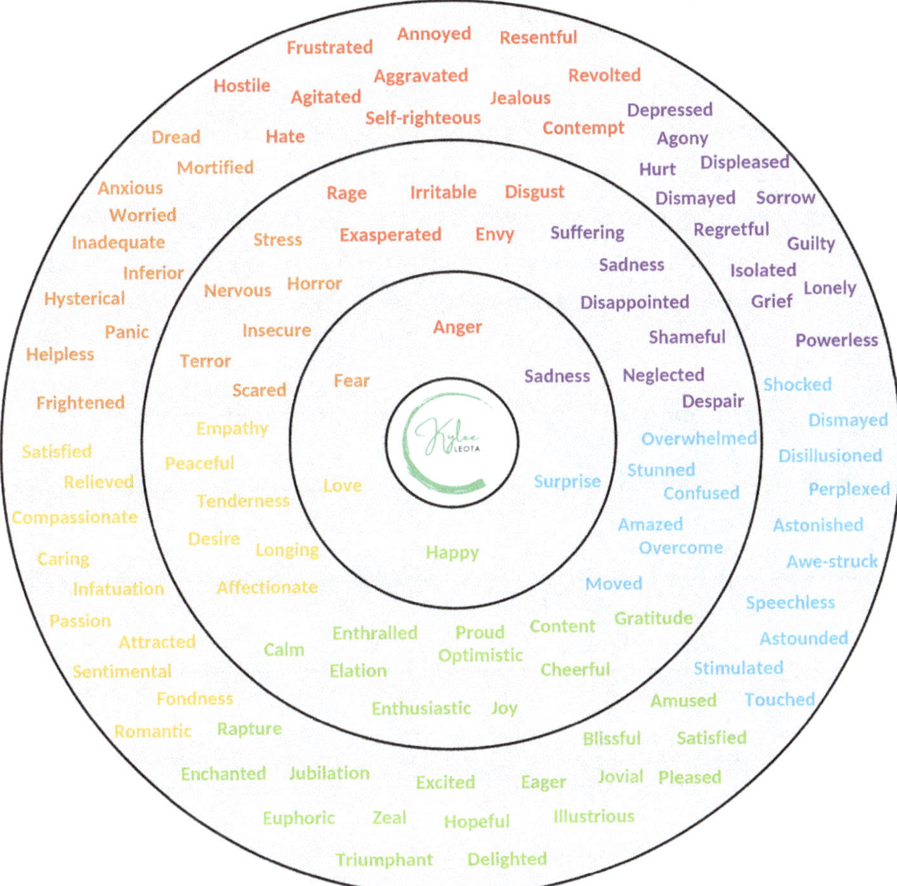

For a printable version of the Emotion Wheel please visit https://elements4success.com.au/resources/.

Naming our emotions accurately is so important because it allows us to find the root cause of our feelings more effectively. Sitting down with an emotion wheel can help you to see that while you might think you're feeling frustrated, what you're actually feeling is disappointed.

Stepping out of your emotions

Once we've identified our emotions, the next action is to step out of them.[64] Removing ourselves from our emotions allows us to see things more objectively. Here's the tool below designed to help you remove yourself from your emotions, and it's important that we do so, because when we reduce the intensity of what we're feeling we can be a little bit more rational in our decision making.

Reflect

Situation	
Thoughts: What is the thought?	
Feelings: What feeling does that bring up?	
Actions: What actions are you taking based on those thoughts and feelings?	
Results: What is the outcome I want?	
Am I getting the outcome I want from these thoughts and feelings	

---

64   David. Emotional Agility.

What is an alternative thought?

Situation	
Thoughts: What is the thought?	
Feelings: What feeling does that bring up?	
Actions: What actions are you taking based on those thoughts and feelings?	
Results: What is the outcome I want?	
Am I getting the outcome I want from these thoughts and feelings	

THE IDEA IS YOU CAN USE USE THIS TEMPLATE TO GAIN CLARITY ON YOUR THOUGHTS AND FEELINGS MANY TIMES AS NECESSARY TO GET TO THE BEST OUTCOME

Walking your why

The third step is called 'walking your why' and this involves using your core values to drive you forward.[65] Whenever you're deciding on what action to take, ask yourself whether the decision reflects your core values. If you have a core value of integrity, you want to ensure that you make a choice that is transparent and fair, for example.

Moving on

The final step is understanding that we can pivot what we're feeling and choose again. David calls this 'moving on'.[66] When you do this you'll

---

65   David. Emotional Agility.
66   David. Emotional Agility.

have the confidence to say, 'Hey, I didn't handle that situation well. I'd like the opportunity to redo that please.' Or, 'Hey, I can see that that decision wasn't the best one. Can we talk this through and maybe make a different choice?' You can then make small purposeful adjustments to align your mindset, values and actions so that you're connected to who you want to be in life and to the INFINITE Leader you want to become.

Now what?

When it comes to nurturing within our INFINITE Leadership journey, one of the conversations I often have with people is, so now what? What do we need to do to be able to apply our awareness and put it into practice? Moving from awareness to action is the heart of emotional intelligence and the nurturing process.

 Reflection Questions

To do this you can start with these reflective questions:

1. What do you notice you are able to be aware of and put into practice as a leader?

2. What are your blind spots that you need to be conscious of? And how does that affect your leadership?

3. On a score of 1-10 what do you give for your ability to demonstrate emotional agility? What does this look like in your leadership journey?

4. What steps am I taking to ensure my values align with my leadership actions?

While there are many more we can examine, this will give you the places to start and the places where you may need to fill in some gaps.

In the coming chapters, we'll continue to explore these principles and see how they intersect with leadership growth and how they can create an environment where individuals can thrive.

'Being able to change your behaviour is central to any personal growth effort, and at the same time it's incredibly difficult, given the power of our unconscious habits. In order to change behaviour to achieve personal growth, we must develop one's capacity: We must develop the ability to create the mental and emotional space inside ourselves to observe and understand, what we are doing, and think about why we are doing it.'

– Beatrice Chestnut

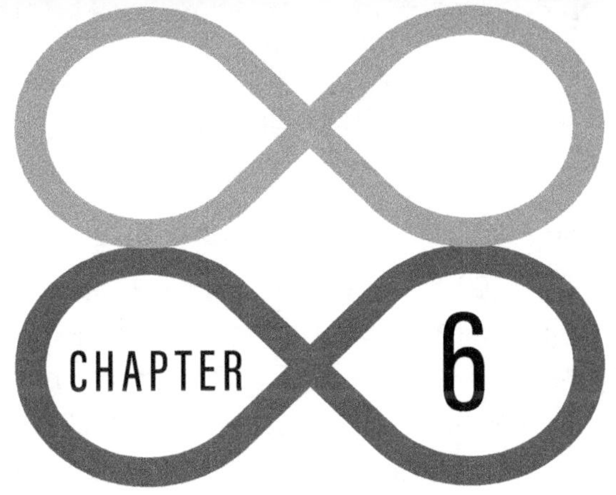

F - FEARLESSNESS

'Love challenges, be intrigued by mistakes,
enjoy effort and keep on learning.'
– Carol Dweck

In the previous chapter, we explored the importance of nurturing ourselves and others to become INFINITE Leaders. We touched on how building trust and emotional intelligence, as well as having a growth mindset, are essential components of this journey. Now we turn our focus to fearlessness.

Fearlessness is often misunderstood. Franklin D. Roosevelt, President of the United States, once said, 'Courage is not the absence of fear, but rather the assessment that something else is more important than the fear.' Nelson Mandela, former President of South Africa also talked about fear saying, 'I learned that courage was not the absence of fear, but the triumph over it. The brave man is not he who does not feel afraid, but he who conquers that fear.'

When we're talking about fearlessness in INFINITE Leadership, we're not talking about having a lack of fear. In fact, we are acknowledging the fact that fear is a real and valid feeling. Instead, what we're saying is that we must take action despite the fear. This means recognising how debilitating fear can be and how the stories we attach to it impact our ability to act during times of fear.

In this chapter, we're going to look at common fears including the fear of failure and the fear of success, how we respond to fear and how the concepts of over-functioning and under-functioning relate to fear and fearlessness. We'll also discuss the SCARF Model by David Rock, and investigate how fear impacts our ability to navigate difficult conversations.

Common fears

When we're talking about INFINITE Leadership, some common fears can hold us back from achieving our goals. And the most common of these are the fear of failure, the fear of success and the fear of discomfort.

The fear of failure

Most people have the desire to be successful. We generally want to do well, and we want to do good. But we also learn through trial and error, which means that failure is actually a vital part of our growth process. So why is it that our brains can be so caught up in the idea that we can't do something wrong – that we need to be perfect, or avoid failure at any cost?

The fear of failure can be extremely debilitating. It can lead to a range of emotional and psychological problems, including perfectionism, depression, anxiety, shame, panic attacks and low self-esteem.[67] And unfortunately, it's a widespread problem with research showing that 31% of adults suffer from it – more than even suffer from fear of spiders.[68] And when we let fear drive us, we miss out.

A CEO who feared failure due to a previous business venture that ended in bankruptcy avoided taking necessary risks in a new company. This avoidance led to missed opportunities for innovation. Through coaching, the CEO learned to reframe failure as a learning opportunity and implemented a culture of experimentation, which eventually led to significant growth and market expansion.

A leader in the nonprofit sector avoided public speaking due to a fear of embarrassing herself in front of donors. After working with a mentor, she took incremental steps, starting with small team meetings and gradually building up to larger presentations. Over time, she gained confidence and realised that even when things didn't go perfectly, the outcome was not as dire as she feared.

Amy Edmondson, a leading researcher in the field of psychology, talks about three different types of failure.

1. **Preventable failures** – these usually involve inattention or a lack of ability and can be prevented by training, rest, checklists or some other solution.

   The Deepwater Horizon oil spill in 2010 is a notable preventable failure that occurred due to a series of missteps and lack of adherence to safety protocols. BP, along with its partners,

---

67 (23 March 2022). Atychiphobia (Fear of Failure). Cleveland Clinic. https://my.clevelandclinic.org/health/diseases/22555-atychiphobia-fear-of-failure.

68 Moline, P. (31 October 2015). 'We're more afraid of failure than ghosts: Here's how to stare it down.' *Los Angeles Times.* https://www.latimes.com/health/la-he-scared-20151031-story.html#:~:text=Fear%20and%20exhilaration%20do%20go,even%20the%20paranormal%20(15%25).

overlooked several warning signs about the integrity of the well and ignored important safety procedures.

The failure could have been prevented through proper training, safety checks and more stringent adherence to protocols. Leadership failure to enforce safety measures and over-reliance on cost-cutting led to the catastrophic oil spill, one of the worst environmental disasters in history.

2. **Unavoidable, complexity-related failures** – these arise because they exist within a complex system, such as aviation or nuclear energy, and occur because of uncertainty inherent in that system. Sometimes failures can be avoided by early identification and correction of small process failures.

   Toyota faced a massive recall crisis between 2009-2010 when reports of unintended acceleration in several of its car models began to emerge. This issue involved a highly complex interaction of systems, including electronics, mechanical pedals and floor mats. While Toyota's manufacturing process is known for its efficiency, complexity related failures arose in the design and integration of different components. Even though the company was able to identify some small process failures, the scale and complexity of modern automotive systems made the issue difficult to detect and avoid in the first place.

3. **Intelligent failures** – these involve hypothesis testing or exploratory testing in an effort to get new knowledge, such as scientific discoveries or market research.[69] In 2014, Amazon's release of the Fire Phone was a commercial failure, as it was unable to compete with established smartphone brands like

---

69 Edmondson, A. (2011). 'Strategies for Learning from Failure.' *Harvard Business Review.* https://hbr.org/2011/04/strategies-for-learning-from-failure.

Apple and Samsung. However, Amazon's CEO Jeff Bezos viewed the Fire Phone as an experiment – an intelligent failure that provided invaluable lessons about the smartphone market and customer preferences. The failure of the Fire Phone allowed Amazon to focus its efforts on more successful ventures, such as Alexa and the Amazon Echo, which became widely successful and paved the way for innovations in voice-assisted technology.

Each of these failures can also impact us on our own leadership journeys. When I was growing up, I can distinctly remember a narrative in my head that said, if I don't try and I don't get the grade, then at least I can say it's because I didn't put the effort in. Yes, this is a preventable failure, but this mindset was also a coping mechanism because one of my greatest fears was putting the effort in and still not achieving what I felt that I should be achieving. So this narrative allowed me to avoid confronting the possibility that I might try my best and still fail.

The problem with this mindset was that my fear of failure ensured that I never really lived past my fears. This caused me to play small for a very long time both personally and professionally. Over the years, and after doing the work, I now acknowledge that the biggest barrier I have is myself and when this fear of failure shows up (which it still does from time to time) I now ask myself what is the worst thing that can happen? And then I have a go anyway, because, as Jeff Bezos showed, if I am learning I never truly fail (intelligent failures for the win!).

Overfunctioning versus underfunctioning

As you can probably tell, I set pretty high standards for myself over the years, often because I was trying to be perfect out of a fear of failing. But when you take this approach, it can lead to a pattern of over-functioning – which is exactly what happened to me.

Brené Brown's concept of over-functioning and under-functioning is closely related to how people respond to fear, stress and anxiety. In her research on vulnerability and courage, Brown explains that when faced with fear or discomfort, individuals often gravitate toward certain behavioural patterns, which can include over-functioning and under-functioning.

Over-functioning refers to a response where individuals take excessive control or responsibility in stressful or fearful situations. They tend to manage, micromanage, or try to fix everything, often stepping into roles beyond their own scope. This pattern is driven by a need to maintain control to manage their anxiety and fear. In leadership, this can manifest as a leader who takes on too much, not delegating, or constantly intervening in others' tasks.

As an over-functioner when things started to go wrong, I would overcompensate, get in and fix things. It gave me a false illusion that I was intentional and productive. In reality I was reacting to a fear of not being good enough.

Over-functioning often stems from people-pleasing tendencies and a need to prove one's worth, and this was certainly the case for me. While it can be a useful strategy in some situations, it can also lead to burnout and dissatisfaction.

Over-functioning can show up in many different ways:

- The fear that things might go wrong or that they will be judged for failure can drive over-functioning. By doing everything themselves, over-functioners try to ensure nothing gets missed and that they avoid criticism.

- Over-functioners can have a hard time embracing vulnerability, which is key to creativity, innovation, and authentic leadership.

By over-functioning, they can avoid asking for help or appearing less competent in front of others.

The need for control is deeply rooted in fear. When leaders feel uncertain or overwhelmed, they may over-function as a way to compensate for the unpredictability of the situation.

Under-functioning is when individuals feel overwhelmed and shut down and so they stop taking action. You'll often see them taking on little responsibility or seeking help or advice excessively. Under-functioners can become so dependent on others that they lose the confidence to function without assistance.

Under-functioners tend to disengage as a way to avoid responsibility or potential blame. By stepping back, they protect themselves from being exposed to risk. They also avoid taking action because they feel inadequate or unprepared to deal with the situation. Their withdrawal is a way to cope with feelings of inadequacy and the fear of being 'found out.'

Some under-functioners avoid decision-making or leadership roles because they fear conflict. By staying passive, they hope to avoid the challenges, confrontations, or tough conversations that may arise in leadership situations.

I've certainly had this experience as well, and it has led me messing up and letting people down because I completely shut down and couldn't seem to accomplish anything. While, for me, under-functioning has been less frequent, it has been equally devastating. And when it occurred it led to a spiral of shame.

When in under-functioning mode, fear can show up in different ways.

- Individuals withdraw, become passive or reduce their level of engagement when facing fear or stress.

- They avoid responsibility, decision-making or taking initiative, relying on others to manage the situation.

- In leadership, this can show up as a lack of direction or disengagement, where leaders don't provide enough guidance, support or action during critical moments.

I think it's important to recognise that there are different kinds of failure, and to take a look at what kinds of fears you might be bringing into your own leadership. If we can recognise the fear, we can learn to switch our mindset to go from the inability to take action (under-functioning) and move into the realm of intelligent failures – that is failures that lead to growth and change.

I certainly recognise with extreme clarity that for many, many years I have had a fear of failure. And while I still have that fear at times, today I'm more open to the fact that I'm on a learning journey which is going to involve false starts and missteps at times. By learning from those missteps we move along the path to becoming INFINITE Leaders.

The fear of success

One of the fears that's less talked about, but is equally prevalent, is our fear of success. This fear involves being so afraid of achievement that people will often sabotage their own successes.[70] In my work I've found that often what people are really afraid of are the consequences of success, rather than success itself. This might be the idea that they'll be given more attention than they want, or will get more work than they

70   Cherry, K. (20 January 2023). 'What Is the Fear of Success?' Verywell Mind. https://www.verywellmind.com/what-is-the-fear-of-success-5179184.

can handle. Or that they'll have to sacrifice or give something else up because of the success.

The fear of success operates subtly, and is more of a subconscious patterning that can be more difficult to recognise. I distinctly remember a moment when I was driving to a holiday destination, listening to *The Big Leap,* an audiobook by psychologist Gay Hendricks and heard him describe the 'upper limit problem'.[71] As explained in Chapter 2, this is the tendency for our subconscious mind to break in with a series of unpleasant or disruptive thoughts to bring us back down to our 'comfortable' level.

As I listened, I felt an uncomfortable truth wash over me. In fact, I was quite literally yelling at the radio, telling it to shut up, because it was hurting my feelings! In that moment I recognised that I had been self-sabotaging my own success and holding myself back all this time because of my own fears and insecurities. But this moment of awareness was just what I needed because it allowed me to actually do something about it.

The upper limit challenges we can face when dealing with success might include:

- Fear of outshining others.

- Fear of losing love or connection.

- Fear that the more successful we become the more responsibility we will need to take on.

- A sense of unworthiness.

- Guilt around success.

- Fear of being perceived negatively.

---

71   Hendricks, G. (2010). *The Big Leap: Conquer Your Hidden Fear and Take Life to the Next Level.* HarperCollins US.

I would add a concept that Brené Brown relates which is the feeling of foreboding joy.[72] We fear feeling joy because we fear it's going to be taken away from us. I believe that we can also fear this in success.

It has taken time, but I'm getting much better at noticing when I'm holding myself back and addressing my own upper limit problem, something we all need to do if we want to become INFINITE Leaders. As Marianne Williamson reminds us, 'Your playing small does not serve the world.' This is not a one and done model. As we embrace the courage required to level up we will constantly be tested and we'll need to consistently respond if we want to see growth.

Understanding our fear triggers through the SCARF Model

It is human nature to want to move away from discomfort. David Rock's SCARF Model identifies that we have things we innately desire to move away from and other things we walk towards. Firstly identifying my own SCARF triggers was another a-ha moment for me, in understanding why I would have different responses as a leader to those around me. It reminded me that everybody views the world through a different lens, and everyone has different motivations for why they do what they do, and these can determine how we interact and how we handle conflict.

In particular, understanding how we respond to fear generally, but specifically the fear of failure and the fear of success, can provide us with valuable insights into behaviour. It can help us navigate how we respond when we are challenged by certain information that triggers our own insecurities or our own motivations.

---

72   Podrazik, J. (18 March 2013). 'Dr. Brené Brown: Joy Is 'The Most Terrifying, Difficult Emotion' (Video).' Huffpost. https://www.huffpost.com/entry/dr-brene-brown-joy-gratitude-oprah_n_2885983.

The SCARF Model

Rock's SCARF Model outlines five domains that influence our responses. These are:

1. **Status** – those with a high status driver might seek validation and recognition. For them, being overlooked or having their work claimed by others could be a significant trigger for fear.

   A leader may fear a perceived drop in social status when they receive feedback that challenges their expertise or decisions. This fear might cause them to avoid learning opportunities or dismiss further feedback opportunities, ultimately hindering personal growth.

   A CEO may hesitate to delegate tasks, fearing that doing so would diminish their authority or influence within the organisation. This could lead to micromanagement and stifle team development, limiting the company's potential for innovation.

2. **Certainty** – some people have a strong need for certainty so they thrive in structured, predictable environments where there is a plan and they know what's going on. When these people are faced with ambiguity or change, this can trigger their fear response.

   A leader may resist making significant life changes, such as switching careers or roles, because the uncertainty of the future drives fear. This fear can result in staying in a comfort zone, preventing personal transformation and the pursuit of new opportunities.

   A senior executive might avoid implementing new business strategies due to uncertainty about their success. The fear of the unknown can lead to stagnation, where they stick with outdated practices even when the company needs transformation to stay competitive.

3. **Autonomy** – those with a high autonomy driver want to have control over their environment and decision-making. If they feel that their ability to make independent choices is taken away, they may feel fear.

   A leader who fears losing control over their personal decisions, such as balancing work and family, might overcommit to one area of life while neglecting the other. This fear can lead to burnout or strained personal relationships.

   In a professional setting, a leader may resist collaborating or working within a team structure, fearing that a loss of autonomy will reduce their influence. This can create a siloed environment, preventing collaboration and leading to disengaged employees who feel excluded from decision-making.

4. **Relatedness** – some people are driven by relatedness, which means that their relationships, social connections and team cohesiveness is really important to them. They may struggle in environments where they feel isolated or where processes are valued over people.

   Personally, a leader might fear not being accepted or liked by peers, which can lead to overcompensating by trying too hard to fit in. This could result in compromised values or decisions, leading to inauthentic relationships and feelings of isolation.

   In the workplace, a leader may struggle with giving difficult feedback, fearing that it will damage their relationships with colleagues. The avoidance of crucial conversations can lead to unresolved issues, team dysfunction, and a lack of accountability within the organisation.

5. **Fairness** – people with a strong driver to fairness value equity and justice. Their fear response can be triggered when they see actions or decisions as unfair.

   A leader may develop a fear of being treated unfairly in social or family situations, such as perceiving an unequal division of responsibilities. This fear can cause resentment, eroding trust and damaging important relationships.

   A fear of unfair treatment might make a leader overly cautious when rewarding or recognising team members, fearing accusations of favouritism. This hesitation can lead to a lack of acknowledgment of high performers, reducing morale and driving disengagement in the workforce.

Rock talks about the fact that we tend to move towards the things that we feel motivated by, and we try to move away from things that do not work for us. Whatever your preferences there is no right or wrong. It is what it is, and being aware of where you sit can help guide your behaviours in a more conscious way.

For example, if you have a high status driver and somebody claims your work as their own, that will be a huge trigger for you. However, if you don't have a status driver, and maybe you have a high relatedness driver, you may not be as impacted by it. If you are highly triggered as a leader, it's important to understand why so you can act in a way that's aligned with INFINITE Leadership.

As another example, I remember presenting the SCARF Model to an organisation where the CEO had a low driver for certainty. He was very spontaneous. He could present whenever, wherever. But while he was very good at going with the flow, his team had a high need for certainty, and this disconnect was causing a lot of tension in their organisation. Once the CEO became aware of how his lack of need for certainty was triggering his team, he was able to take action to remedy those concerns and build a better-functioning team. In doing so, he embraced INFINITE Leadership.

In yet another example, I have a strong autonomy driver, though if you asked me, I wouldn't have thought so. But as I reflected over the years, and looked back into my career in the government, I realised that I actually did. At the time I was working in a role where I was able to be quite autonomous in how I delivered my work and how creative I was in my solutions to get to the desired outcome. And as I reflected I realised that this was probably the reason I lasted so long in that role in the first place.

So how do you figure out what your driver is? And how do you figure out what the drivers of your team members are? It's important to understand this because understanding our primary drivers and those of our team members helps us navigate fear-triggering situations more effectively. If you have a team member who has a high certainty driver, that means that, when you need to have a meeting with them, you don't have an impromptu conversation. It means you put it in the calendar and potentially set an agenda so that they feel more safe and secure, and are able to be more present in the meeting.

How to find your fear drivers

As you were reading above, did anything resonate? Which fear drivers made you feel uncomfortable as you read them? Note these down, and how you typically react when you find these fears triggered. This will help you to understand what actions to take for you to move along your INFINITE Leadership journey.

What happens when we face fear?

There's been a lot of research into fear and what happens when we're confronted with it. In fact, when we are confronted with fear our brain initiates one of four primary responses – fight, flight, freeze and fawn. These are essentially stress responses that govern how your body reacts to danger.[73]

1. **Fight** – your body's way of facing any perceived threat aggressively.

2. **Flight** – your body urges you to run from danger.

3. **Freeze** – your body's inability to move, act or react to a threat.

4. **Fawn** – your body's stress response to try to please someone in order to avoid conflict.[74]

But what we also know is that, when we are moving into a point of fear or stress, the way that our brain processes information is impacted, including our executive functioning skills, and this also impacts how we show up as a leader.[75]

Executive functioning skills and fear

Your executive functioning skills are like the air traffic control tower in your brain. And just like a real air traffic control tower monitors how planes take off and land, the one in your brain processes how you

---

73   Taylor, M. (24 June 2024). 'What Does Fight, Flight, Freeze, Fawn Mean?' WebMD. https://www.webmd.com/mental-health/what-does-fight-flight-freeze-fawn-mean.

74   Taylor. What Does Fight, Flight, Freeze, Fawn Mean?

75   Sklar, M. (9 March 2018). 'Getting Past Fear.' Executive Functioning Success. https://executivefunctioningsuccess.com/getting-past-fear/#:~:text=Sources%20of%20Fear&text=The%20stress%20of%20these%20%E2%80%9Clittle,to%20manage%20time%20and%20life.

give and receive information and how you internalise that information. In other words, your executive functioning system manages how you handle stress and fear. And when this system is overwhelmed, it becomes challenging to think and act rationally.

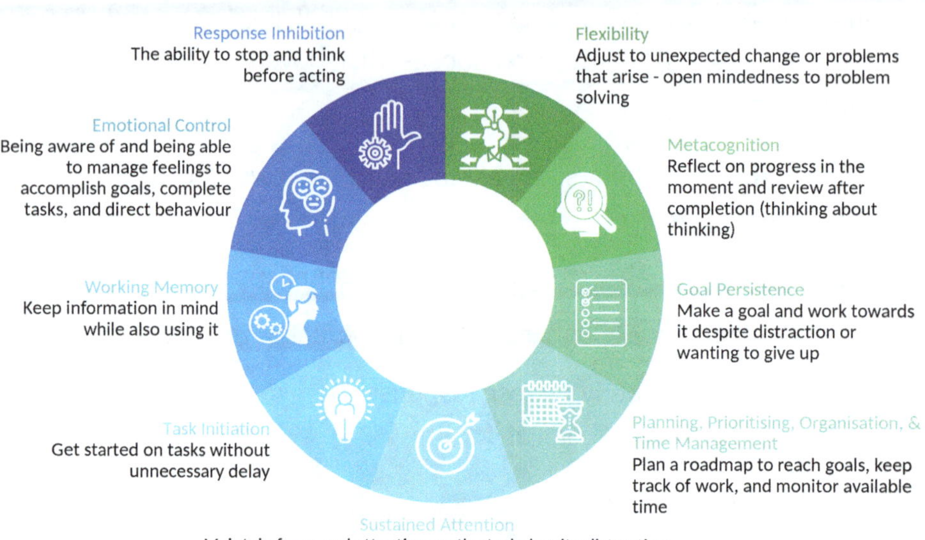

One of the ways you can assess your fear response is by reflecting on how you behave when you are calm versus when you are stressed.

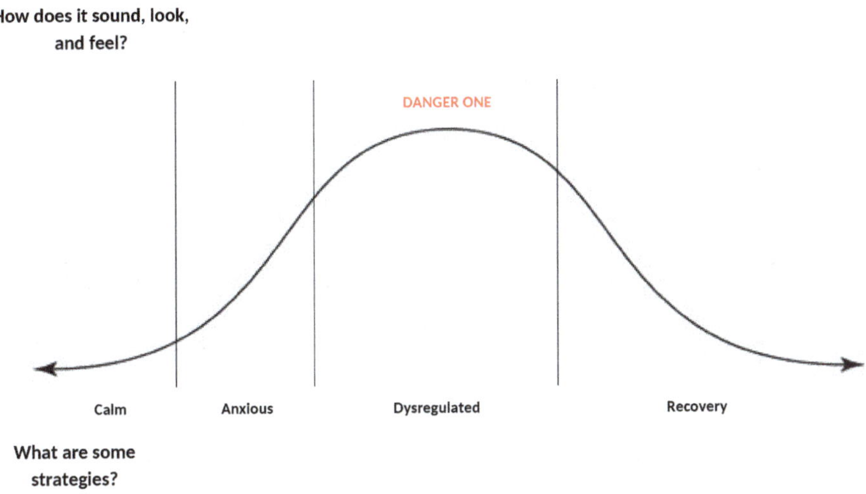

Do you lose your ability to manage situations? Or are you still able to function effectively? What rating out of 10 would you give yourself when you're calm? What about when you're feeling overwhelmed and stressed? Getting this insight will help you identify where you might have an executive functioning skill deficit.

Moving towards fearlessness

Fearlessness is not about eradicating your fears completely, but about moving forward despite them. It involves acknowledging fears, understanding their roots and building skills and capacity to manage those fears rather than allowing yourself to be hijacked by your emotions. As an INFINITE Leader, being able to model this movement towards fearlessness is one of the greatest gifts we can give to those we lead.

Adopt fear-setting exercises

Consider conducting a fear-setting exercise rather than just goal-setting exercises. Tim Ferris designed this tool, not only to identify fears, but also to prepare to move through these fears, with actionable steps.[76]

The exercise is simple and involves asking yourself a series of questions.

1. What is the worst thing that can happen? What exactly could go wrong?

2. What could you do to prevent the worst-case scenario from happening?

3. If the worst happened, what repair could you implement?

4. What are the potential positive outcomes if you succeed?

This process allows you to move through fear, rather than being hijacked by a risk-averse mindset. It also helps remind you to focus on what is within your control rather than focusing on what is out of your control.

---

76   Ferriss, T. (15 May 2017). 'Fear-Setting: The Most Valuable Exercise I Do Every Month.' Tim Ferris. https://tim.blog/2017/05/15/fear-setting/.

Be a buffalo, not an ostrich

INFINITE Leaders face fears like a buffalo, not an ostrich.

Running from the
storm

Head in the sand

Buffalo's running
toward the storm

Most animals run from a storm, attempting to escape it, but the water buffalo takes the opposite approach, they move directly toward the storm. By doing so, they reduce the time spent in discomfort and emerge on the other side more quickly. This simple yet profound behaviour mirrors what great (INFINITE!) leaders do when faced with fear and challenges. Rather than avoiding difficulties, they charge toward them, understanding that confronting fear head-on leads to faster growth, greater resilience, and the opportunity to emerge stronger.

In leadership, fear is inevitable. Whether it's the fear of failure, fear of making tough decisions, or fear of navigating the unknown, it can often be tempting to avoid these challenges in the hope they'll resolve on their own. But avoidance, like running from the storm, often prolongs the discomfort. Leaders who postpone difficult decisions or avoid addressing critical issues only end up allowing those problems to fester, increasing their negative impact. By moving directly into fear – like the buffalo charges into the storm – leaders not only shorten the period of uncertainty but also create opportunities for growth and learning.

Charging into fear builds resilience. Just as the buffalo grows stronger by facing the storm, leaders develop mental and emotional strength by confronting challenges rather than running from them. Leadership is a journey filled with storms, and those who practise leaning into fear and discomfort become more equipped to handle future challenges. Every time a leader faces a crisis, tough decision or personal doubt and moves through it, they add to their capacity to lead with greater calm and confidence the next time.

On the other hand, when they attempt to run away and avoid the storm, they end up spending more time under its dark clouds. Problems become bigger, relationships deteriorate and opportunities slip away.

Running toward the storm doesn't just benefit leaders – it has a ripple effect on their teams and organisations. Leaders set the tone for how fear and challenges are handled. When leaders consistently avoid problems, teams pick up on that avoidance, which can foster a culture of indecision and risk aversion. But leaders who embrace challenges, demonstrating that fear is part of the process and acting with courage, encourage a culture of resilience. Teams learn to see challenges as opportunities for growth and respond to adversity with action rather than avoidance.

Charging toward the storm enables faster transformation. Leaders who act quickly in the face of challenges set themselves and their organisations up for faster recovery and greater long-term success. When issues are addressed early, before they spiral out of control, leaders are able to transform setbacks into breakthroughs. Like the water buffalo, they move through the storm and emerge stronger, more agile, and ready to take on whatever comes next.

In leadership, as in life, storms are inevitable. The water buffalo's wisdom reminds us that the key to success and resilience is not in avoiding fear but in charging straight into it. Leaders who embrace this approach move through challenges faster, grow more resilient, and inspire others to do the same. It is in the storms that true leadership is forged.

 ## Reflection Questions

To help yourself move towards fearlessness, you can ask yourself the following reflection questions:

1. How is fear of failure stopping you from being the leader you aspire to be?

2. How is fear of success stopping you from being the leader you aspire to be?

3. What do you need to move towards that you are currently moving away from?

4. What important conversation is fear stopping you from having? What steps do you need to take to be able to have it? What is the consequence of inaction?

By examining these questions, you can begin to shift your mindset from fear-driven reactions to purposeful, courageous actions. In doing so, you are taking crucial steps towards becoming the INFINITE Leader you aspire to be.

'Innovation distinguishes between a leader and a follower.'

– Steve Jobs

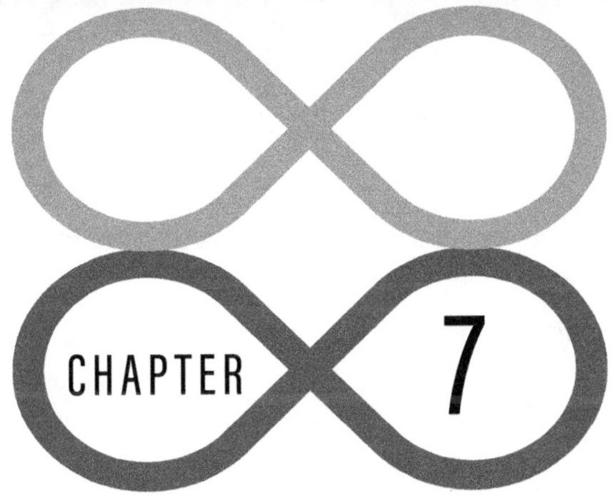

I – INNOVATION

'Creativity is thinking up new things.
Innovation is doing new things.'

– Theodore Levitt, Economist and Harvard Business School professor

In the previous chapter we explored fearlessness, learning how to adapt this into our own INFINITE Leadership. Now we shift our focus to innovation. But what is innovation? It's certainly a word we hear bandied about a lot in the business world, and the traditional definition is simply 'a new idea, method or device'.[77] But as leaders, innovation is not just about creating something new. It's also about being willing to challenge the status quo, rethink existing ways of doing things and, of course, foster a culture in our teams and organisation that encourages creative thinking generally. And to truly be an INFINITE Leader, you must be able to challenge the status quo and innovate.

Influential economist, Joseph Schumpter, highly regarded for his work

---

77   Merriam-Webster. (n.d.). Innovation. In Merriam-Webster.com dictionary. https://www.merriam-webster.com/dictionary/innovation.

on entrepreneurship and innovation, emphasises that innovation is more than just invention. It is the implementation that significantly improves or transforms markets, industries or practices.[78]

Clayton Christensen's work on disruptive innovation expands on Schumpeter's ideas and is often cited in business leadership literature. In his book, *The Innovator's Dilemma*, he defines innovation as the creation of products and services that eventually disrupt existing markets by providing new value.[79]

Peter Drucker, another leading thinker on innovation and leadership, describes innovation as the 'systematic effort to create purposeful, focused change in an organisation's economic or social potential.' Drucker's work emphasises innovation as the primary way organisations grow and maintain competitive advantage.[80]

In my experience with INFINITE Leadership, innovation comes as a result of dealing with doubt and being willing to face hard conversations. As Brené Brown teaches us, the birthplace of innovation is vulnerability.[81] And as she also says, vulnerability is not a weakness – it's actually the cousin of courage.[82]

When we're vulnerable, we're more open to accepting that we might need some help. We feel that we're in a safe space to unpack the things that

---

78 Schumpeter, J. (1942). *Capitalism, Socialism and Democracy.* Harper & Brothers.

79 Christensen, C. (1997). *The Innovator's Dilemma: When New Technologies Cause Great Firms to Fail.* Harvard Business Review Press.

80 Drucker, P. (1985). *Innovation and Entrepreneurship: Practice and Principles.* Harper & Row.

81 Walters, H. (2 March 2012). 'Vulnerability is the birthplace of innovation, creativity and change: Brené Brown at TED2012.' TEDBlog. https://blog.ted.com/vulnerability-is-the-birthplace-of-innovation-creativity-and-change-brene-brown-at-ted2012/#:~:text=Culture%20TED%20Talks-,Vulnerability%20is%20the%20birthplace%20of%20innovation%2C%20creativity,change%3A%20Bren%C3%A9%20Brown%20at%20TED2012.

82 Walters. Vulnerability is the birthplace of innovation, creativity and change.

we may need to learn, unlearn and even relearn when we find that we're not getting the outcomes we want. This allows us to consider our unique frame of reference, which might have developed from things in our identity, like our stories and the narrative we've built around our experiences.

In this chapter, we'll explore the nature of innovation, the importance of rethinking and how to pivot to change the outcomes we're getting as well as how to maintain an environment that's conducive to innovative practices. And all of this is an essential part of your INFINITE Leadership journey.

Why innovation matters in INFINITE Leadership

In INFINITE Leadership, inspiring creativity is crucial for team success – but it starts with the self. Leaders who innovate cultivate their own creativity and curiosity. They give themselves the space and opportunity to think differently, explore new possibilities and break free from old ways of thinking. A self-innovating leader might engage in creative exercises like journaling, mind mapping or seeking out new experiences that spark their imagination. This practice helps them come up with fresh ideas for personal and professional growth, which they can apply in both their leadership and personal lives.

Innovation is essential in leadership because it drives growth, adaptability and long-term success. In the journey toward INFINITE Leadership, innovation becomes the catalyst for not just solving today's challenges but for continually evolving and striving toward a higher level of excellence. Leaders who embrace innovation create the conditions for continuous improvement and growth, both for themselves and those they lead.

In INFINITE Leadership, innovation is not merely a tool for progress – it is the driving force that unlocks the potential for continuous excellence in both personal and professional leadership. By embracing innovation, leaders transcend challenges, create value and inspire greatness in themselves and others. Making innovation the cornerstone of their leadership approach allows you to push the boundaries of what's possible, fostering a culture of continuous improvement and building a legacy of excellence that benefits everyone.

The following table demonstrates how innovation can be a tool for progress in both your personal and professional lives and the areas it can impact for the better.

PERSONAL	Leading Transformational Change	
	Innovation leads to transformation, not just in organisations but in personal leadership journeys. Leaders who innovate in self-leadership continuously transform their own thinking, behaviours, and approaches. By embracing this type of personal innovation, leaders set the foundation for greater personal fulfilment and the ability to lead transformational change in others.	*Self-leadership example:* A leader might undergo a major mindset shift by adopting a growth mindset, as described by Carol Dweck, leading to a transformation in how they approach challenges. This innovation in self-leadership helps them become more resilient and adaptable, fuelling greater success for themselves and their teams.
	Creating Personal Value	
	In leadership, innovation creates value for stakeholders. In self-leadership, it creates value for yourself. By innovating, you continually increase your personal worth – whether that's through developing new skills, enhancing your emotional intelligence, or expanding your capabilities. Self-innovation ensures that you are always growing and contributing at your highest potential.	*Self-leadership example:* A leader might focus on improving their emotional intelligence by learning from experts like Daniel Goleman and Timothy R. Clark. Through this self-innovation, they increase their ability to empathise, connect, and lead with compassion, creating more value in both their personal and professional relationships.
	Enhancing Personal Decision-Making	
	In leadership, innovation enhances decision-making by providing new tools and perspectives. In self-leadership, innovative thinking helps you make more effective personal decisions. Leaders who embrace self-innovation are better equipped to weigh options, think critically, and make choices that align with their long-term vision of success.	*Self-leadership example:* A self-innovative leader might use techniques like Tim Ferriss' fear-setting exercise to improve their decision-making process. By considering worst-case scenarios and preparing accordingly, they become more confident and effective in making bold, growth-oriented decisions.

<table>
<tr><td rowspan="4">PERSONAL</td><td>Inspiring Creativity in Others</td><td>Leading Transformational Change</td></tr>
<tr><td>INFINITE Leadership is not just about personal growth but about inspiring others to innovate and think creatively. Leaders who model innovation create a ripple effect, encouraging their teams to be bold, experiment, and challenge the status quo. As leaders, fostering creativity in others helps establish a culture of collective excellence, ensuring that innovation permeates every level of the organisation.</td><td>*Self-leadership example:* Transformative leaders don't just adapt to change; they drive it. They challenge the existing paradigms and lead their teams through major shifts that redefine the future. Innovation allows INFINITE Leaders to transform their organisations, ensuring they are always moving toward new possibilities and higher levels of achievement.</td></tr>
<tr><td>Creating Value for Stakeholders</td><td>Enhancing Decision-Making</td></tr>
<tr><td>Innovative leaders constantly seek ways to create value for customers, shareholders, and stakeholders. In INFINITE Leadership, creating value goes beyond immediate returns – it is about establishing long-term trust and loyalty. By driving innovation, leaders can ensure that they deliver lasting value, positioning their organisations for sustained excellence in the future.</td><td>*Self-leadership example:* Innovation enhances decision-making by encouraging leaders to embrace diverse perspectives and explore new possibilities. INFINITE Leadership is about making strategic, informed decisions that propel organisations forward. Innovative leaders are able to cut through complexity and ambiguity, ensuring that their choices drive progress and continuous improvement.</td></tr>
</table>

<table>
<tr><td colspan="2"></td></tr>
</table>

Adaptability to Change

In a world where industries and technologies are rapidly changing, leaders must innovate to stay agile. By creating an environment that encourages adaptability, leaders foster resilience in their teams, enabling them to navigate new challenges and opportunities. INFINITE Leadership demands this flexibility – it is about continuously evolving and driving improvement even in the face of uncertainty. When leaders innovate, they build the necessary adaptability to thrive in an ever-changing landscape.

Problem-Solving with a Fresh Perspective

Leadership example: Innovative leadership encourages leaders to approach problems with fresh, creative solutions. Whether it's rethinking business models, improving processes or enhancing customer experience, innovation fuels new ways of thinking. INFINITE Leadership is about not settling for the status quo. It's about constantly seeking better, more effective solutions that propel leaders and their teams toward excellence.

Driving Continuous Improvement

Innovation is the foundation of continuous improvement. In INFINITE Leadership, the pursuit of excellence is never ending. Leaders must constantly look for new opportunities to improve, grow and evolve. Innovation ensures that this progress is sustainable. Leaders who cultivate innovation are able to push boundaries, constantly reimagining what's possible and ensuring their organisations and teams continue to excel.

Boosting Employee Engagement and Ownership

Leadership example: When leaders foster a culture of innovation, employees feel empowered to contribute ideas and actively participate in driving change. This sense of ownership and responsibility directly enhances morale and engagement. INFINITE Leadership is about creating a culture where everyone feels they have a voice, where innovation is a shared value, and where individuals take ownership of the organisation's journey toward continuous excellence.

Staying Ahead of the Competition

In competitive markets, the ability to innovate is a game-changer. INFINITE Leaders not only keep up with industry trends but also anticipate them. By staying ahead of the curve, they ensure their organisations lead the way, rather than simply reacting to external forces. The ability to foresee and act on future opportunities is what sets INFINITE Leaders apart—they innovate to maintain their competitive edge, ensuring sustained growth and success.

Building a Culture of Trust and Safe Risk-Taking

Leadership example: Innovation thrives in environments where leaders foster trust and allow safe risk-taking. INFINITE Leadership is about leading by example—showing teams that failure is part of the learning process and that experimentation is critical to growth. By encouraging calculated risks, INFINITE Leaders cultivate an environment where innovation is celebrated, and where teams feel supported to think outside the box and push for new ideas.

PROFESSIONAL

Barriers to innovation

While innovation is critical for continuous improvement and excellence, leaders often face barriers that prevent them from driving creative solutions and transformative change. Understanding these barriers allows leaders to address them head-on, creating a culture where innovation can thrive.

Below are five common barriers to innovation that frequently hold leaders and organisations back.

1. Fear of failure

Fear of failure is one of the most significant barriers to innovation (as well as to our general ability to lead well, as seen in the Fearlessness chapter). Leaders who have a fear of failure often hesitate to try new things due to the risk involved. This fear can paralyse decision-making, causing leaders to default to what feels safe rather than exploring innovative solutions.[83]

In INFINITE Leadership, we recognise that failure is part of the growth process. Leaders who overcome this barrier create environments where experimentation and learning from mistakes are encouraged, ultimately driving progress and excellence.

2. Resistance to change

Resistance to change is a major obstacle in leadership. Whether from teams or the leaders themselves, the comfort of familiar methods can prevent innovation from taking root. Innovation requires a willingness to let go of established norms and embrace new possibilities.[84] Leaders

---

83 Edmondson, A. (2019). *The Fearless Organization: Creating Psychological Safety in the Workplace for Learning, Innovation, and Growth.* Wiley.

84 Kotter, J. P. (1996). *Leading Change.* Harvard Business Review Press.

must model this openness to change and encourage their teams to do the same. In INFINITE Leadership, the ability to drive change is essential for continuous improvement and long-term success.

3. Lack of resources

Innovation requires investment – whether it's time, money or talent. One of the most common barriers leaders face is the lack of resources to execute innovative ideas. Without proper support, even the best ideas can fall flat. Leaders must advocate for the resources necessary to drive innovation and ensure that creative solutions can be implemented. In INFINITE Leadership, resourcing innovation is an investment in continuous improvement and the future of the organisation.

4. Short-term focus

The pressure to deliver short-term results can undermine long-term innovation efforts. When leaders are focused solely on immediate gains, it limits the time and space for experimentation, making it difficult to invest in the transformative projects that drive future growth. To cultivate innovation, leaders must balance the demands of short-term performance with long-term strategic vision. In INFINITE Leadership, creating excellence means having the courage to look beyond the short-term and commit to lasting progress.

5. Lack of Psychological Safety

Innovation thrives in environments where people feel safe to take risks and share new ideas.[85] If leaders do not foster a culture of psychological safety, employees may hesitate to propose innovative solutions out of fear of criticism or failure. Leaders must create a space where teams feel confident to voice their ideas without fear of repercussions. In INFINITE

---

85   Clark, T. (2020). *The 4 Stages of Psychological Safety: Defining the Path to Inclusion and Innovation.* Berrett-Koehler Publishers.

Leadership, we know that psychological safety is essential to driving innovation and empowering teams to push boundaries.

6. Lack of self-worth

Self-worth is a big one. It's hard to be creative and think outside of the box when we don't think we have anything to offer. Often it's our own stories or the narratives that play out in our minds that might hold us back. We might unconsciously choose to play small due to internalised beliefs about our own abilities or capabilities.

There is no one in the world exactly like you, so who are you not to be great? The world deserves to hear your thoughts, to experience your creativity and to understand what you know. So embrace your self-worth.

7. Reactive state of being

Often leaders can spend too much time in a reactive state. This is where you're spending all your time catching the balls that are being thrown at you (responding to external stimuli), rather than positively and proactively driving change.

If you take a moment to audit your day, how often would you find yourself reacting rather than proactively acting? What do you need to do in order to shift towards a more proactive mindset?

8. Emotional hijacking

I see it all the time – extraordinary people being hijacked by their emotions or their own dysregulation. When this happens to a leader, it can stifle their ability to think clearly and innovate. Understanding your own behaviour cycle and recognising the signs of emotional dysregulation – such as being easily overwhelmed, acting impulsively or having angry outbursts – is the key to staying in the optimal zone for innovation.

How can we better innovate for INFINITE Leadership?

It starts with rethinking

We've spoken about the power of reflection in our practices, and the same holds true when it comes to innovation. Part of innovation is really about the idea of rethinking. If you want to have more impact as a leader, you need to constantly test your thinking to ensure that you're creating ideas and concepts that bring about a positive change in you, in your team and in your organisation.

When we go through the process of rethinking, we gain new information. And as you gain new information you have the right, and I'd say the responsibility as an INFINITE Leader, to change your mind if what you've been doing no longer meets your needs. As the saying goes, 'If you do what you always did, you'll get what you always got!' We must understand that innovation is acknowledging when our existing methods are no longer serving us and be open to change.

To create an environment that fosters innovation we've got to get buy-in and establish a sense of belonging. Again this comes from having safe spaces where we support ourselves and our people to have a voice. This leads me to the concept of the thermostat versus the thermometer.

The thermostat versus the thermometer

What does this have to do with INFINITE Leadership? A thermometer reflects the environment around it. When the temperature changes, so does the reading. In contrast, a thermostat sets the temperature – it defines the climate, controls the environment and shapes the conditions around it. This distinction is pivotal in understanding how leaders can drive innovation both within themselves and in the people they lead.

Have you ever entered a room where the temperature is dull, cold and tense, and you find yourself feeling exactly that way as well? Or maybe you've gone into a room that's full of energy and fun, and you've found yourself feeling energetic as well? Many leaders, particularly those who are more empathic people, will find themselves absorbing the energy around them, both positive and negative. This certainly applies to me.

However, to be truly innovative and truly INFINITE Leaders, we must act as the thermostat rather than the thermometer. This means that we need to be the one that determines the energy in the room, setting the tone and creating an environment that encourages that innovation.

As leaders, we need to be thermostats, intentionally setting the direction and tone for innovation, rather than merely reacting to external forces. When we operate as thermometers, we're subject to external pressures, challenges or the moods of others, leaving little room for proactive leadership. This reactive approach creates an environment where innovation stagnates, because we aren't actively shaping the conditions that allow creativity and new thinking to thrive.

Leaders who function like thermometers often struggle to establish a culture of continuous improvement. They reflect the status quo, react to daily crises and, as a result, innovation is either slow or non-existent. This holds back both personal and organisational growth because without intentional leadership, the conditions for improvement never evolve.

Being unaware of this dynamic can leave you in a passive state, allowing your environment to dictate your actions. This reactive leadership stifles the kind of innovation that is crucial to long-term success, both for yourself and for the teams you lead.

When we're innovating, we have to have the power to be the thermostat, not the thermometer. But what does that mean in practice? Imagine that you're running at 50 degrees – that's pretty hot. If you surround yourself with people that are operating at 30 degrees, you run the risk of lowering your own 'temperature' especially if you don't take steps to increase their own temperatures. If you're surrounded by people that are also operating at about 50 degrees, you might just stay where you are. Neither of these situations are good for innovation.

But what happens if you surround yourself with people that are operating at 80 degrees, either because this is their natural temp, or because you've helped them to raise their temperatures? Now you've got a choice. You can either elevate your own level to match theirs, or you can lower yourself to maintain your own comfort.

As an innovator, the choice is obvious. If you can sustain the higher level and make this the new normal, then you will be in a much better position to innovate. But this requires making a conscious choice and a commitment to stay in control of your energy and focus. The difference between those people that are making significant changes is the length of time that people stay at the new level despite perhaps feeling uncomfortable in this new space. Our goal ultimately is to elevate ourselves to be operating at a higher level, more frequently and over a longer time.

Many leaders reinforce this thermostat mindset. John C. Maxwell, in his *21 Irrefutable Laws of Leadership*, emphasises the 'Law of Influence,' which aligns directly with the idea of setting the temperature.[86] True leadership, according to Maxwell, is about creating a vision and shaping the culture, not simply reflecting it. Simon Sinek, in *Leaders Eat Last*, advocates for leaders to build a 'circle of safety', which echoes the importance of leaders setting the environment – one where innovation and risk-taking are possible.[87]

Jim Collins, in *Good to Great*, provides another perspective, highlighting that great leaders consistently shape the environment by implementing disciplined, strategic actions.[88] Those who fail to do so are merely reacting to external pressures, much like thermometers. These insights all align with the principle that leaders need to drive innovation through intentionality, not by passively accepting the current state of affairs.

Of course, we also need to consider our environment, and what we're subjecting ourselves to. Part of being an INFINITE Leader is being able to reflect on how what we're doing is acting on ourselves, and our own identities. We certainly don't want to subject ourselves to things that might be detrimental to our wellbeing – such as overwork or long hours – simply to elevate our levels. The crux is always to be conscious of ourselves and what is happening to us while pushing boundaries around innovation.

---

86   Maxwell, J. (2022). *The 21 Irrefutable Laws of Leadership: Follow Them and People Will Follow You.* HarperCollins Leadership US.

87   Sinek, S. (2017). *Leaders Eat Last: Why Some Teams Pull Together and Others Don't.* https://www.amazon.com.au/Leaders-Eat-Last-Together-Others/dp/0670923176/ref=asc_df_0670923176/?tag=googleshopdsk-22&linkCode=df0&hvadid=712259705004&hvpos=&hvnetw=g&hvrand=12146349733838661638&hvpone=&hvptwo=&hvqmt=&hvdev=c&hvdvcmdl=&hvlocint=&hvlocphy=9069129&hvtargid=pla-324956558057&psc=1&mcid=1b97ca483db93e9a9c6661511966444e&gad_source=1.

88   Collins, J. (2021). *Good To Great.* CENTURY - TRADE.

So how do we start to elevate our innovation levels?

1. Be intentional.

2. Set a culture both personally and professionally of curiosity and experimentation.

3. Empower leaders at all levels.

4. Innovate your own personal leadership growth (remember is it about continuous improvement and continuing to evolve as a leader).

5. Model the way.

It continues with consistency

As an INFINITE Leader, innovation is how we lead into a better future. And to achieve this we're always trying to operate at more optimal levels. But to 'optimise' our leadership, we must first be consistent.

Too often as leaders we're looking to find or jump into the extraordinary. But we shouldn't overlook the simplistic things that we do everyday that help us be innovative and, ultimately, extraordinary.

Consider how Mark Zuckerberg wears the same clothes every day.[89] He says it's because it saves him from decision fatigue, so he's able to save his energy for more innovative thinking around the things that really matter in his work and life. He takes out the low hanging fruit around decision making and harnesses his energy and time into things that he sees as important.

---

89 Yerunkar, A. (13 May 2024). 'Why Genius Like Einstein, Steve Jobs, Zuckerberg Wear Same Outfit Everyday? Know The Reason, Which Can Help You.' India. com. https://www.india.com/business/why-genius-like-einstein-steve-jobs-zuckerberg-wear-same-outfit-everyday-knowing-the-reason-which-can-help-you-6924839/.

When it comes to your own consistency, what are the simple routines and rituals that allow you to be innovative in areas of your life that are important to you? Are there some that you could implement to let you maintain your focus on and mental energy for innovation? Are there decisions or actions that you could automate that will leave you more free to embrace creative thinking?

If so, I encourage you to adopt them – and when you do so, you'll be in a better space to innovate.

Remember, ordinary things done consistently create extraordinary!

Your zones of operation

To truly foster an innovative mindset in yourself, you need to be aware of the zones in which you operate. These are the calm zone, the anxious zone, the danger (or dysregulated) zone and the recovery zone (first discussed in the last chapter).

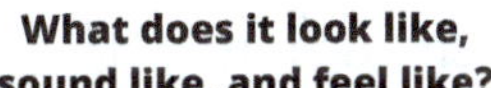

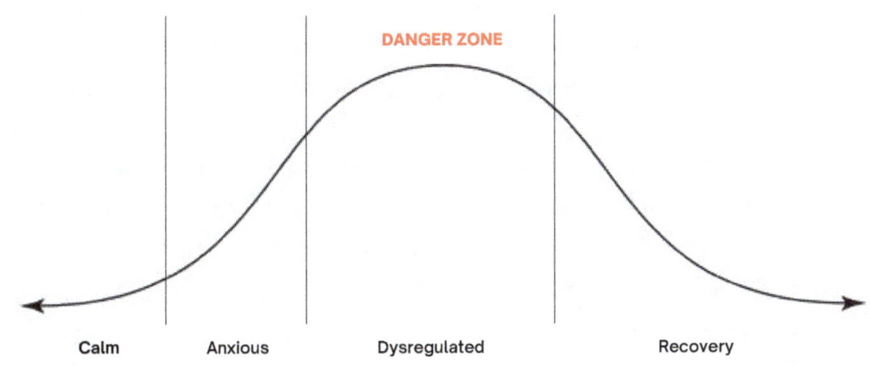

**What are some
  strategies?**

1. **Calm zone** – When you're in your calm zone, you're feeling regulated. You're feeling in flow. You're feeling optimal in everything that you do.

2. **Anxious zone** – As we start to move along the path to elevated innovation you will notice that things become a little more stressful. This is when you're in a little more of an anxious state. That doesn't necessarily mean you have anxiety. It means you're a little bit more heightened, a little bit more stressed. And it feels like there's a little bit of pressure on you.

3. **Danger (Dysregulated) zone** – As we move into what I call the danger zone or the dysregulated zone, your heightened stress starts to look like overwhelm. You begin to feel under the pump, with sometimes overwhelming feelings of fatigue. In this zone, some people can begin to exhibit a lack of emotional control. This could mean emotional outbursts, like blowing up, or for others it could be a complete shutdown, where they withdraw from the task at hand and find they're not completing the things that they need to.

4. **Recovery zone** – If you've found yourself dysregulated, you must then work to move yourself into the recovery zone. This takes time. And the minute we try to do too much, too early, we then send ourselves right back into that dysregulated zone.

To be an INFINITE Leader who is ready to lead innovation, you need to be continuously bringing yourself into the calm zone. What does that look like, sound like and feel like for you? Now consider what it looks like, feels like and sounds like when you're in your anxious zone, your dysregulated zone and your recovery zone. And what strategies do you currently utilise to help keep you there in your calm zone? What strategies do you have when you notice that you're feeling anxious to move yourself back to calm, and what strategies do you currently have if you get dysregulated?

Regularly completing the activity above has helped me remove dysregulation from my life by nearly 90% because it helped me realise that I wasn't capturing these zones early enough in the process, and that meant that I could never really get back to the calm zone. I was always stuck in reactive, feeling overwhelmed and burnt out, and then I'd be reacting, trying to pull myself up by the socks and trying to get myself out of it.

But by being proactive and recognising the signs earlier, I was able to stay in the calm zone, or move back from my anxious zone into the calm zone much quicker. This helped me significantly reduce emotional hijacking in my life. This change has led to improved outcomes in my ability to innovate – both personally and professionally – and to lead others to do so as well. It has also allowed me to let things go that no longer served me, and not get so attached to things that were bothering me and that means moving more strongly into INFINITE Leadership.

The Innovation wheel

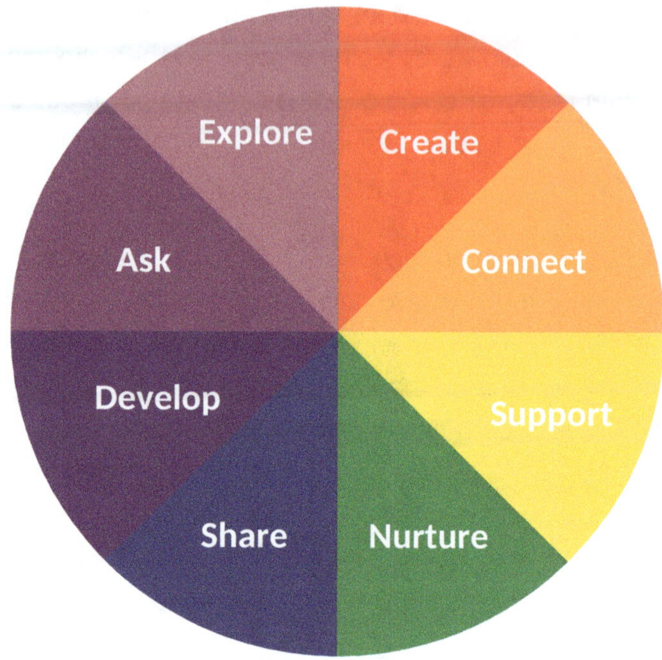

The concept of an innovation wheel which was developed in the 90s represents a holistic approach to innovation that integrates different stages of ideation, development, collaboration and nurturing support. It encourages leaders to engage in all stages rather than focusing only on ideation or execution. When leaders feel stuck, the wheel provides a structure to assess which area — asking questions, connecting with others or nurturing an idea — may need more attention to move forward. INFINITE Leadership requires innovative practices at every level. And before you say that you are not innovative, below are a number of ways to approach innovation. There are many pathways to innovation – work to your strengths and find a style that works for you. Embrace and encourage the innovative style of your team, and look for complementary approaches that will give you depth in your team and organisation.

Here's how can it work in your innovation journey, both personally and professionally

1. Share

Personal Self-Leadership: Sharing in personal leadership involves being open with others about your goals, challenges and lessons learned. For example, if you're working on improving your resilience, you might share your progress with a trusted friend or mentor to gain feedback and insights.

Professional Leadership: In a team setting, a leader might share their vision with the team, ensuring everyone understands the direction and purpose behind a project. This could involve sharing data, strategies and expectations transparently to align the team's efforts. It should also involve encouraging your team to share their thoughts and ideas.

2. Develop

Personal Self-Leadership: Personal development focuses on building your skills and knowledge. This could involve setting aside time to take a leadership course, improving a soft skill like communication or developing emotional intelligence to lead yourself more effectively.

Professional Leadership: In the professional context, developing others is key to leadership. A leader might create opportunities for team members to upskill, such as offering mentoring or workshops, or delegating tasks that help employees grow in their roles.

3. Ask

Personal Self-Leadership: Asking powerful questions is vital for self-awareness. For example, regularly asking yourself, 'What can I do differently?' or 'What's holding me back?' can unlock insights that drive personal improvement.

Professional Leadership: Leaders can cultivate a culture of curiosity by asking their teams thought-provoking questions. They may ask, 'How can we improve this process?' or 'What obstacles are you facing that we haven't addressed?' These questions empower others to contribute ideas and foster a collaborative environment.

4. Explore

Personal Self-Leadership: Exploration involves seeking out new perspectives and experiences. You might explore different leadership styles by reading books, attending workshops or observing other leaders you admire to gain a broader understanding of leadership.

Professional Leadership: In a team setting, a leader may encourage exploration by allowing employees to experiment with new approaches to projects. This could mean adopting an innovation mindset by exploring alternative methods of solving problems or allowing time for creative brainstorming sessions.

5. Create

Personal Self-Leadership: On a personal level, creating opportunities for innovation involves taking initiative. You might create a new routine, journal for clarity on your leadership challenges or set up a personal vision board to track your progress and goals.

Professional Leadership: Professionally, leaders create opportunities for innovation within their teams. This could involve developing a new product, spearheading a process-improvement initiative or creating a new framework for collaboration, enabling the team to generate fresh ideas.

6. Connect

Personal Self-Leadership: Personal leadership requires connecting with people who can inspire or challenge you. This could involve expanding your personal network to meet mentors or joining a leadership forum or mastermind group where you can engage with like-minded individuals.

Professional Leadership: A leader facilitates connection within their team by fostering collaboration. This could be done through cross-departmental meetings, organising team-building activities or simply ensuring open lines of communication so team members feel heard and supported.

7. Support

Personal Self-Leadership: Supporting yourself might involve practising self-compassion during tough times, or seeking support from a coach or counsellor to help you work through leadership challenges.

Professional Leadership: Leaders demonstrate support by providing the necessary resources and backing for their team members. This can include offering emotional support, mentoring, providing constructive feedback or ensuring employees have the tools and training they need to succeed.

8. Nurture

Personal Self-Leadership: Nurturing yourself could mean cultivating a growth mindset by regularly reflecting on your experiences and learning from them. It could also involve taking care of yourself through mindfulness practices, exercise or ensuring a healthy work-life balance.

Professional Leadership: Professionally, nurturing can be about fostering an environment where innovation and creativity can thrive. Leaders nurture their teams by encouraging personal development, providing opportunities for growth and creating a psychologically safe space where team members feel comfortable sharing ideas and taking risks.

By taking these steps you'll find that you're in an excellent position to adopt and leverage innovation personally and for your team and organisation to allow you to elevate your INFINITE Leadership.

What's next?

In this chapter we've covered the crucial role that innovation plays in your INFINITE Leadership journey. We know it's not just about introducing new ideas but also about challenging the status quo, embracing vulnerability and creating environments that allow us and our teams to embrace creativity. Through innovation we can inspire transformative change and drive long term success.

If you're still wondering where you are on the innovation pillar, ask yourself the following questions. The answers to these will guide your next steps – and don't forget to seek support if you need it!

 # Reflection Questions

1. When do you notice that you are the thermometer rather than the thermostat? How do you pivot in those instances?

2. In what ways have I adapted or changed my leadership approach in the last year? How could I be more flexible and adaptable?

3. How does the culture of my organisation either support or stifle innovative thinking? What steps can I take to enhance an innovation-friendly environment?

4. Am I rewarding and recognising innovation in my team? If not, what changes can I make to ensure innovative efforts are acknowledged?

As we move forward into Chapter 8, we'll explore the concept of nobility in leadership and how it can serve to shape your ability to build trust and foster growth within your team and organisation.

'Innovation distinguishes between a leader and a follower.'

– Steve Jobs, Co-founder of Apple Inc.

N - NOBILITY

'The best way to find yourself is in the service of others.'
– Ghandi

Nobility may seem like a concept from a bygone era, evoking images of knights and royalty. But the essence of nobility is highly relevant in business today, particularly when you're on the path of INFINITE Leadership.

In order to create effective and sustainable leadership, we need to redefine nobility as a commitment to integrity, humility and service of others. Nobility in leadership is about building others up, rather than pushing people down. Noble leadership is sustainable leadership and when you push people down you risk drowning them, which is certainly not sustainable. But when we're acting as noble leaders we're focused on building others up because we recognise that when we lift people up we collectively rise.

If you're searching for noble leadership, it must begin with self-awareness. Being a noble leader means cultivating a mindset of service. It means prioritising the growth and wellbeing of others. It is both compassionate and involves accountability. And it's the difference between seeing leadership as a technical problem to solve and seeing it as a human-centred endeavour that requires continuous self-assessment and reflection.

Ryan Holiday, famous for marrying stoicism and marketing theories, captured this idea well when he said, 'Ego is what keeps you from helping others to thrive.' The challenge for you as a leader when you're looking to rise to the level of an INFINITE Leader is that you will need to set your ego aside and create spaces for creative conversations, innovation and capacity building within your team. You must be open to the idea that you don't have all the answers. And you must be willing to get help. Whether that means finding a coach or a mentor, fostering open communication or engaging in that all-important self-reflection.

There's no place for ego in leadership, yet it constantly features in most areas. Noble leaders are curious leaders that always start from a position of compassion, giving people unconditional positive regard. They assume that people are doing the best they can, with what they have. That does not mean condoning poor behaviour, but it does allow us to believe that when you know better, you do better.

Why noble leadership matters to INFINITE Leadership

Noble leadership is the heartbeat of INFINITE Leadership because it transcends personal ambition and focuses on driving continuous improvement for everyone. It's about leading with integrity, humility and the genuine desire to uplift those around you – not for personal gain, but for the long-term success of the entire team and organisation. Noble leaders are committed to something greater than themselves.

They don't lead for recognition. They lead to create environments where everyone can excel and grow.

In INFINITE Leadership, noble leadership ensures that the focus isn't just on short-term wins or self-centred achievements. Instead, it's about building something sustainable and enduring. Noble leaders model trust, empathy and accountability, which in turn inspires those around them to give their best, fostering creativity and resilience. This approach helps create a leadership ecosystem where everyone has the opportunity to thrive, and excellence becomes not just an outcome, but a standard.

I believe that one of the noblest acts you can do is hold space for someone else's thoughts. Too often we struggle to actively listen to another's perspective, particularly if it is different to our own, because we are too busy crafting our responses to truly listen to understand. Holding space for others' perspectives doesn't mean you necessarily agree or condone their thoughts. However, making someone feel seen and heard goes a long way towards being able to ensure the other person will hear you when you have something important to say.

Being able to lead with understanding perspectives is a skill that enables leaders to find a unifying order even when one is seemingly non-existent. It helps us take a big picture stance to see things clearly.

The commitment to noble leadership also ties back to the principle of continuous self-awareness and growth. Leaders who prioritise nobility are not afraid to confront their weaknesses or seek feedback. They lead with the understanding that their role is to empower future leaders, leaving behind a legacy that goes beyond individual accomplishments. Noble leadership is the catalyst that ensures the journey toward excellence is not just about personal success, but about lifting everyone along the way.

Barriers to noble leadership

Even the most committed leaders will face barriers to noble leadership. But recognising the things that can hold you back is the first step in overcoming them.

Ego

One of the most common obstacles to noble leadership is your own ego. If you become too focused on status, power or success you can start to see other people as obstacles rather than collaborators, and other people's ideas as roadblocks rather than opportunities. Ego in leadership is also associated with a lack of empathy and poor decision making, neither of which is going to help you achieve your goal of noble leadership.

Research shows that ego-driven leadership can have a huge negative impact on a team's culture.[90] It can lead to decreased morale, a loss of trust and poor communication and it can stifle innovation (another pillar of INFINITE Leadership). It can also cause higher turnover rates.

Fear of vulnerability

Noble leadership requires vulnerability – this means that you acknowledge your mistakes, can and do ask for help and admit that you don't have all the answers. But when we're afraid of looking weak, incompetent or unprepared we aren't able to embrace our vulnerability. And that stops us from connecting to others and our own noble leadership.

---

90   Gleeson, B. (n.d.) 'The Leadership Dichotomy Of Ego And Humility.' *Forbes.* https://www.forbes.com/sites/brentgleeson/2024/04/05/the-leadership-dichotomy-of-ego-and-humility/.

Inconsistent values

When leaders demonstrate inconsistent values – that is they say one thing but do another – it creates mistrust and uncertainty and undermines nobility. Inconsistency between what you say you value and what you actually do, damages any culture of respect and honour that you can build otherwise.

Lack of self-awareness

We've already touched on self-awareness in this chapter and earlier in the book, but it bears repeating. Without self-awareness, leaders may not realise when their actions are being driven by ego, fear or inconsistency. This lack of insight can lead to leadership behaviours that aren't part of noble leadership.

Failure to adopt an authentic culture of accountability

The problem with accountability is that historically it has been seen as an excuse to treat people poorly, get rid of people and make people feel awful about themselves as humans. As leaders, we might find this type of culture holds us back from becoming truly noble leaders.

On the other hand, when authentic accountability is implemented, it is a noble act. It is about supporting people to be better. It is about doing right over being right, and working towards a win-win outcome for everyone involved. It focuses on the problem, not the person, but equally and ultimately helps people to be better today than they were yesterday.

Developing nobility in your leadership – A.L.E.A.D.E.R. Model

Leaders on an INFINITE journey need to understand how to develop their own noble leadership. This starts with giving yourself permission to be noble.

Permission to be noble

A prerequisite for taking any action to bring nobility into your leadership is the process of giving yourself permission to lead with nobility. Granting yourself the permission to be noble opens up possibilities for growth, both for yourself and for your team.

Make a list of three things that you will do once you give yourself permission to be a noble leader, and then use this list to guide your future actions. This may be amended by the information you take in during the rest of this chapter, but it's the act of writing it down that gives you the permission to embrace nobility. Now you just build and amend from here!

A.L.E.A.D.E.R. Model

If you're looking to develop more nobility in your leadership, and overcome any barriers holding you back, consider starting with the A.L.E.A.D.E.R. Model.

A – Assessment – The first step is to step back and assess the current state of your leadership. Look at your actions, interactions and decisions and consider whether you're demonstrating integrity, humility and service in each of these instances. If not, why not?

L – Learn – Continuous learning is a huge part of leadership. Throughout your leadership journey, seek out feedback from both your team members and your own leaders. Ask them directly whether they see you demonstrating integrity, humility and service. Learn from this feedback and from your successes and failures within your leadership. Take those learnings onboard and adapt your leadership approach as necessary. Nobility is about acknowledging that you don't know everything and being willing to grow.

E – Element – Identify the key elements of noble leadership, which likely include honesty, transparency and the willingness to serve others. How do these elements and the other elements you've identified show up in your leadership? For example, do you create a culture of respect and trust within your team? Do you have open communications? Do those around you feel able to openly discuss challenging issues with you?

A – Awareness – As we've already touched on, self-awareness is crucial to noble leadership. It is ongoing throughout the learning process. Be mindful of when your ego is driving your actions rather than a commitment to integrity and service. In moments of pressure or crisis, check in with yourself. Ask yourself whether you're still leading with integrity despite the pressure. If not, how can you recalibrate?

D – Do – Do you take actions that align with the noble leadership principles you've identified? These actions could be giving yourself permission to be vulnerable, acknowledging when you need help or taking steps to build up and lift up others within your team.

E – Engage others – One of the best ways to ensure that you're acting in alignment with principles of nobility is to engage your team in conversations about nobility in leadership. Ask them what they think this means, and listen when they describe their perspectives. It's important to create safe spaces where team members feel valued and heard as well. Encourage an open dialogue, where ideas can be shared without fear of judgement.

R – Reflection – Just like in the earlier stages of INFINITE Leadership, self-reflection is vital. Regularly reflect on your leadership journey. What are the barriers preventing you from embodying noble leadership more consistently? How can you address these barriers?

Creating a culture of respect, trust and honour in your team

Creating a culture of respect, trust and honour in your team is an essential part of noble leadership, and an essential part of your journey to becoming an INFINITE Leader. When team members feel respected and valued, they're far more likely to engage fully, open up and share their ideas and buy in to common goals. But creating this culture requires you to take intentional action.

So how can you do that?

1. **Lead by example** – The foundation of any respectful culture is the idea of mutual respect and that means it starts with you. Your behaviour sets the tone for the entire team, so you need to demonstrate respect for others in all your daily interactions. Show humility to your team, admit when you're wrong and be open to feedback from both those you're responsible to and those you're responsible for.

2. **Establish clear values** – Define the core values around nobility that you want to guide your team's behaviour. Even better, develop these values in collaboration with your team. Communicate these values regularly and integrate them into

all your decision-making while encouraging your team to do the same.

3. **Build trust through transparency** – Trust is built through consistent, open and honest communication. Share information with your team – or share how information can easily be found or accessed. Be transparent about the organisation's direction and decision-making process as well as your own.

4. **Create safe spaces for dialogue** – as mentioned previously, encouraging open communication where team members feel safe expressing their ideas and concerns means that they'll be more likely to contribute meaningfully. As part of this, address conflicts quickly and constructively and do your best to make sure that everyone's voice is heard.

Leading with integrity through pressure

Every leader will have to deal with moments of pressure or crisis, even you. But when you're in a pressure situation it's easy to deviate from your values. Noble leadership, however, demands that we hold onto our integrity despite any internal or external pressures or stressors. This means that we must stay true to our commitments, act with integrity and always consider the impacts of our decisions on others.

To lead through pressure be sure to stay grounded in your values. This will stop you from taking impulsive decisions or actions that are driven by pressure rather than real, high-value information. If you tie your decision-making to your core values, you'll know that you can never be too far off from the noble choice. If you're struggling, get support. You don't have to handle everything on your own – not even truly INFINITE Leaders are capable of that. Instead, look for input from trusted colleagues, advisors, coaches and mentors who can provide a new perspective and support.

By seeking support you also show that you value others' insights, and this humility and openness is central to noble leadership.

Learning to lead with nobility

As we've seen, noble leadership is not about grand gestures or titles. It's about the small, consistent actions that build others up. It involves setting ego aside, being true to your values and creating an environment where others can thrive.

If you want to discover whether you're on the right road to embracing noble leadership as part of your INFINITE Leadership journey, start by using the below reflection questions as a guide. They will help you to explore and deepen your noble leadership practice. Remember that noble leadership is an ongoing journey that requires self-awareness, intentional action and the courage to serve others selflessly.

 Reflection Questions

1. How do I define nobility in my own leadership practice?

2. In what ways do I demonstrate integrity, humility and service in my leadership role?

3. How do I create a culture of respect, trust and honour within my team or organisation?

4. In moments of pressure or crisis, how do I ensure that I lead with integrity and ethical responsibility?

5. What are the barriers preventing me from embodying noble leadership more consistently, and how can I address them?

Now that you've embraced your noble leadership, it's time to move onto the next pillar or your INFINITE Leadership journey – and that's the leadership favourite... influence.

'Leadership is not about being in charge. It is about taking care of those in your charge.'

– Simon Sinek

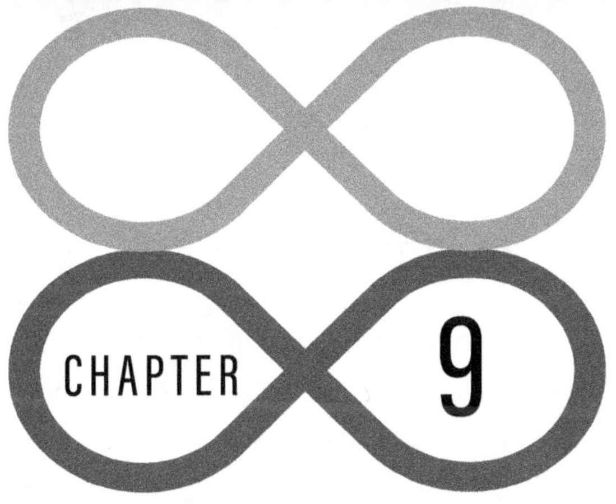

I - INFLUENCE

'A leader is anyone who takes responsibility for finding the potential in people and processes and who has the courage to develop that potential.'
– Brené Brown

Influence is the next stage in our INFINITE Leadership journey. It plays a pivotal role in shaping the culture and outcomes of your team and organisation.

In this chapter we'll explore what influence is and the why and the how of influence – why it matters to INFINITE Leadership and how to recognise and overcome barriers and foster a culture where you can influence effectively for a strong culture and team growth.

The essence of influence

Influence is about more than simply getting others to agree with your ideas and decisions – that's totalitarianism. Instead, influence is about building relationships, creating psychological safety and fostering an environment where open dialogue, creativity and collaboration thrive. Jim Collins said it very well when he said, 'True leadership only exists if people follow when they have the freedom not to.'

You can think of the essence of influence as the difference between transactional and transformational influence.[91] Transactional influence is what is used in top down, hierarchical organisations and is focused on the tasks that need to be done. On the other hand, transformational influence is rooted in empathy, and leaders who practise it rely on encouragement and support to motivate and inspire others.

To create true transformational influence, INFINITE Leaders must go beyond 'hierarchical' power dynamics where you lead simply because you are in the position of the leader. Instead, true influence comes from seeing it as an opportunity to inspire and elevate everyone they interact with.

High-performing leaders understand as well that their influence can and should extend in all directions, and vice versa. It must extend upward to those whom they report to. It needs to extend downward to those who report to them. It needs to extend across to their peers and colleagues. And it needs to extend outward, across the wider organisation and even external stakeholders.

---

91   Laker, B & Patel, C. (29 August 2020). 'Strengthen Your Ability to Influence People.' *Harvard Business Review.* https://hbr.org/2020/08/strengthen-your-ability-to-influence-people.

When you can influence in all directions, you're really able to foster a shared vision, build a cohesive team and drive change. And this is the catalyst for change.

Why influence matters for INFINITE Leadership

When it comes to INFINITE Leadership, influence is the driving force that allows you to develop and guide your team to grow and thrive and create collective success. Influence matters because it is the catalyst for change. It creates the momentum needed to propel individuals and teams towards shared objectives and true collaboration.

When we truly understand and leverage influence, we can then model behaviours, set standards and establish trust within our teams, which is a vital part of being an INFINITE Leader. I have seen good people get stalled in their leadership journey despite great ideas and practices, because they could not create the influence needed to implement.

Barriers to influence

Like all the pillars, there are things that hold us back from creating real influence. But recognising these obstacles is the first step to overcoming them.

Lack of psychological safety

One of the most critical components of influence is psychological safety. If individuals don't feel safe to express their opinions, challenge ideas or give and receive feedback, influence becomes virtually impossible.

When your team doesn't feel psychologically safe, they might become withdrawn, silent and disengaged so they can avoid conflict. And in this situation, you won't be able to effectively influence your team, or likely anyone else.

Ineffective communication

Influence relies on clear, intentional communication, particularly when we're under stress. Misunderstandings can easily arise when we don't adapt our communications styles to the listener and the situation, or when we don't recognise the need to listen ourselves. And when we're stressed, communication can become rushed, vague or even defensive, and this will impact your ability to convey the shared vision and get buy-in and support.

Unconscious biases and behaviours

Every leader – yes even an INFINITE Leader – has conscious and unconscious behaviours that can drive our decisions and impact our ability to influence others. This might be your body language, the tone of voice you use, and even the way you think others want to receive information (which likely aligns with how you would like to receive information). If you don't embrace self-reflection and become aware of these biases and unconscious behaviours you could unknowingly create barriers that prevent others from engaging with you authentically. And this will impact your ability to influence.

Misalignment of strategies

How you influence is not one-size-fits-all. Your strategy for influence needs to flexibly adapt to match individual people and teams in terms of the preferences they have for receiving feedback and support, as well as delivering opportunities and strategies for capacity building. As a leader, if you apply a single strategy across the board, without considering individual needs, you risk losing the trust and respect that you need in order to be a transformational leader.

How to create a culture of influence

Creating a culture of influence is not about exerting power over others – it's about inspiring them to take action, share ideas and work towards common goals and outcomes. To do this INFINITE Leaders need to create an environment where every team member feels valued and heard. Your influence grows when the people in your organisation believe that you're behaving authentically, trust you and feel safe to express themselves without judgement or repercussions.

So, when it comes to how to create a culture of influence, this includes creating a culture of psychological safety, embracing effective communication, leading the way with your own actions and behaviours and ensuring that your strategy for influence is flexible and adaptable.

The foundation of influence – psychological safety

At the heart of influence lies psychological safety. Amy Edmondson gives us this definition. She says psychological safety is 'the belief that one will not be punished or humiliated for speaking up with ideas, questions, concerns, or mistakes, and the team is safe for interpersonal risk taking.'[92]

____

92   Edmondson. The Fearless Organization.

Psychological safety is the key to influencing change. You cannot influence change if you can't have honest, open, and transparent conversations. And you can't have these kinds of conversations unless you feel comfortable speaking up. This is what psychological safety delivers.

Project Aristotle was a major initiative by Google on its quest to build the perfect team. What they discovered was that there were five major components to the 'perfect team', and who was on the team mattered less than how they interacted.

These five vital components included dynamics, structure and clarity, meaning, dependability and impact. However, what the research also showed was that there was one crucial underlying dynamic, and without it, all others were irrelevant. That dynamic was psychological safety.

When people feel that they're in a psychologically-safe culture, influence becomes a two-way street. Team members are then open to being influenced and feel empowered to contribute their own perspectives. On the other hand, when teams don't feel safe, you will start to see a high turnover. One organisation I know, which struggled with a toxic culture, lost 33 staff within an 18-month period. This saw them lose significant momentum and also damaged their credibility as a leader in their field.

Psychological safety is not about 'being nice' or letting things go. In fact, the safest environments are the ones that have all four levels of psychological safety, including inclusion safety, learner safety, contributor safety and challenger safety.

> '1. Inclusion Safety – members feel safe to belong to the team. They are comfortable being present, do not feel excluded, and feel like they are wanted and appreciated.

2. Learner Safety – members are able to learn through asking questions. Team members here may be able to experiment, make (and admit) small mistakes, and ask for help.

3. Contributor Safety – members feel safe to contribute their own ideas, without fear of embarrassment or ridicule. This is a more challenging state, because volunteering your own ideas can increase the psychosocial vulnerability of team members.

4. Challenger Safety – members can question and even challenge others' (including those in authority) ideas or suggest significant changes to ideas, plans, or ways of working.'[93]

So, it's not about not 'fighting' but learning how to 'fight well'. The safest environments allow people to speak up and challenge the status quo. People feel confident that they can do that without fear of losing something. At the end of the conversation, people know they're going to be okay. Too often I see this fail when people don't have good communication systems and protocols in place to 'fight well'.

Building a psychologically-safe culture involves adopting a few key elements, personally and organisationally.

1. Be authentic, not tokenistic

When you're developing psychological safety, it's important to be authentic, not tokenistic. In fact, authenticity is absolutely crucial. If your actions are perceived as tokenistic or insincere, your team will very quickly lose all trust in you.

---

93   Geraghty, T. (15 June 2021). 'The Four Stages of Psychological Safety.' PsychSafety. https://psychsafety.co.uk/the-four-stages-of-psychological-safety/.

On the other hand, when you're authentic – when you acknowledge your own vulnerabilities – then you show that it's okay to be imperfect. And that encourages others to feel and be open and honest as well.

A tokenistic approach to psychological safety is dangerous and is one of the fastest ways to break trust and destroy the connections around you. In organisations, this is the epitome of a toxic culture.

2. Do the work on yourself

Do the work on yourself first. If you cannot tolerate people challenging you, or have trouble listening to others, you will struggle to implement psychological safety. No one is going to want to follow a leader who doesn't work on their own vulnerabilities and communication, doesn't respond well to feedback, and fails to listen to others. You need to be sure that you're doing the internal work to understand how you're creating a psychologically-safe culture yourself and, where you're falling down, take steps to remedy that.

3. Empower conversations

A key element to psychological safety is empowering open, brave, and courageous conversations. Ask yourself, 'As a leader, how do I create safe spaces for conversations?' INFINITE Leaders will be creating spaces where each person feels empowered and even encouraged to share their thoughts, ideas, and concerns. To really take these to the next level, you should be asking for input from those in your team on how feedback should be given and received. And yes, you should be prepared to receive feedback as well!

Remember from Chapter 4, about Identity, we know that we all have different communication preferences. Some people like the bullet point versions. Some like the softer approach. Take responsibility for yourself. Just as organisations have the responsibility to provide safe spaces to work, you also have a responsibility. What does inclusion, learner, contribution and challenger safety look like to you? What do you need in order to give these to your team and organisation? Equally, what do you need in order to receive these from others? And have you communicated that?

It's important to reflect on what you need in order to engage in this process wholeheartedly. What do you need to be aware of that could potentially impact how you show up in this space? Having honest conversations with yourself as a leader, of self and others, is the foundation of INFINITE Leadership.

It is important to remember that having psychological safety is not the end game, creating excellence is.

4. Focus on the big picture

In any discussion around psychological safety, it's important to keep the bigger picture in mind. This is especially relevant when it comes to feedback. How often do we actually ask people how they would like to give feedback, and how often do we ask them how they would like to receive feedback?

If the goal of feedback is to improve outcomes, we need to keep this aligned with the big picture, and that includes the feedback we give. Ask, what is the outcome we seek? How can I deliver that in a way that the person who needs to adjust their behaviour will receive it?

Sue Anderson, in her book *Feedback Fitness*, identifies several things that get in the way of us being able to engage effectively in feedback, including protective armour to protect ourselves from our emotions.[94] And let's be honest – because feedback has historically been done poorly, we often have big emotions as both the giver and receiver of feedback. Other fears include damaging the relationship and trying to do it perfectly.[95]

Sue says to ask great questions to understand ourselves and our own stories around feedback. If we understand ourselves and our responses, we are likely to be more grounded in feedback conversations, regardless of whether we are the giver or receiver.

5. Get support

If your team or organisation has struggled with creating psychological safety, or you have a toxic culture, changing it may be challenging. You may need an outside facilitator to get it right, at least in the beginning. An INFINITE Leader will seek out support from facilitators, coaches or consultants who can provide them with the right tools and guidance to begin to create a psychologically safe space.

As with almost anything, outsiders can offer objective perspectives and help facilitate difficult conversations. This can reset the tone of your team or organisation for healthier workplace culture. As a leader, my growth amplified when I had a trusted outsider who could hold space for my thoughts and feelings, enabling me to process and recalibrate back into action.

---

94   Anderson, S. (2024). *Feedback Fitness.* Good2gr8 Coaching.
95   Anderson. Feedback Fitness.

Building influence through effective communication

Psychological safety might be the first and most crucial part of creating influence, but effective communication falls close behind. Learning how to communicate and interact must become an integral part of your standard operating procedure. But to do it well – in line with INFINITE Leadership – you need to be able to communicate with intentionality, clarity and adaptability.

- *Intentionality* – When you communicate with intention you convey your message in a way that aligns with your desired impact (or how you want to influence). This can involve taking time to consider how best to communicate so there is an alignment between the two.

- *Clarity* – Clear communication involves being mindful of not just what you say but also how you say it.

- *Adaptability* – Adaptability means that your communications are tailored to those that you're speaking to.

Leaders must also understand that communication is not limited to just the words that we're saying. In fact, scholars estimate that nonverbal communication accounts for 60-90% of total communication.[96] This is body language, eye contact, facial expressions and even gestures.[97] Effective communication relies on us being able to interpret those elements of nonverbal language to determine the intention behind the communication.

---

96   Lorié A et al. (25 September 2017). 'Culture and nonverbal expressions of empathy in clinical settings: A systematic review.' Patient Education Counselling. https://pubmed.ncbi.nlm.nih.gov/27693082/.

97   Mahler, L. (2024). *Gravitas: Timeless Skills to Communicate with Confidence and Build Trust.* Wiley.

To master the art of speaking and listening – which is the crux of INFINITE Leadership communication – you need to adapt your style to the situation and the communication preferences of those you're communicating with. This also puts you in an excellent position to better handle challenging conversations.

I worked with a leadership team that had undertaken a massive shift after working through the identity work (Chapter 4). We had unpacked many things, including communication and feedback preferences and conflict resolution styles. As I met with one of the team, she opened up about how upset she was with another member of the team. She had told her about a really important meeting that she needed her to attend and she hadn't shown up. This not only triggered frustration and resentment but also the feeling of being let down.

As we dug deeper, I asked her to reflect on the information she already knew from the work we had done. What was her communication preference? Email. They were beautifully constructed, which took a lot of time and effort, because of her perfectionistic tendencies. The person she really needed at the meeting, what was her communication preference? NOT email! In our group session, she said, 'I know I should be better at emails, and I am working on it, but if you need me to do something, the BEST thing you can do is come and tell me face to face and say THIS IS IMPORTANT!'

So where did this fall down? If the person wanted the team member at the meeting, did she need to ensure she communicated her preference? Or was it the responsibility of the team member to make sure attended? Or was it the responsibility of both parties? These issues will continue to be perpetual problems if we do not understand and acknowledge those preferences. Here the leader had done the work to understand herself and her preferences, but had missed the opportunity to influence because she hadn't adapted her communication style to what the team member needed. This demonstrates why ongoing commitment to doing the work is so important.

Model the behaviours

One of the most powerful ways to influence others is through your own actions. Leaders must model the behaviour they wish to see because it's their behaviour that sets the standard for the team and signals what is valued within the organisation.

I was sitting with a client who was experiencing frustration with the performance of her team. She stated that she openly told them it was okay for them to express their opinion on things. In fact, she encouraged it. But only one in her 20 direct reports ever spoke up.

I asked her how her meetings usually went. She told me they generally started by her giving the state of play and then mostly everyone agreeing with her.

I asked if she thought her team felt that way because they valued her opinion. Then I suggested a different approach. 'What if instead of giving your opinion first, you asked for their input and really listened? What would you be modelling then?'

The conversation continued, and I learned more about her leadership style. When I asked if she took lunch breaks, she admitted that she rarely did, even though she encouraged her team to take breaks. So I asked, 'What are you modelling for your team when you don't take care of your own wellbeing?'

One of the five keys to exemplary leaders according to Jim Kouzes and Barry Posner is to model the way.[98] Daniel Goleman and Cary Cherniss also identify modelling as one of the five ingredients to successful organisational leaders.[99]

As the leader I encourage you to reflect – in the moment if you can or set aside some time each day – and ask yourself, what did I model today? Did I act intentionally to model what will increase the performance of my team? If yes, how can I build or maintain this in my practice? If not, how did I miss the mark and what am I going to do differently? If you are not showing up and modelling the way, and need help to move forward, I encourage you to reach out and seek support.

This is just as true in personal leadership as it is in your professional life. If you want your children to communicate without yelling, do you communicate in a calm way? Many of us grew up in the generation of 'do what I say, not what I do', but as the evidence suggests, this is a highly ineffective way to create influence. In fact, it most often has the opposite effect.

Influence is not dictated but demonstrated. If you want to foster a culture of trust and transparency that will allow for influence, you need to start by reflecting on how you interact with your team. Are you approachable? Do you listen without interrupting? Do you admit when you don't have all the answers?

Your actions set the tone for your team. When you model openness, transparency and respect, you create an environment where others feel comfortable following suit. Remember, what you do as a leader is more influential than what you say.

---

98   Kouzes, J & Posner, B. (10 February 2023). *The Leadership Challenge: How to Make Extraordinary Things Happen in Organizations*. Jossey-Bass.

99   Goleman, D & Cherniss, C. *Optimal: How to Sustain Excellence Every Day*. Penguin (General UK).

Embrace a flexible and adaptable strategy

A key aspect of creating a culture of influence is recognising that you must be flexible and adaptable at all times. This means that you're flexibly meeting the unique needs of the individuals that you're looking to influence as you push for change and growth within the overall team.

As a leader, you must remain open to adjusting your strategy based on who you're communicating with and the outcomes that you're looking to achieve. This will lead to real influence. On the other hand, a rigid and inflexible approach often leads to misunderstandings, which can then lead to a loss of trust and diminish your influence.

Flexibility in influence means that you're willing to change your communication style, your feedback methods and even your approach to problem solving. It does not mean that you change your core values or your overall long-term vision for the organisation. But it does mean that you take into account when a team member might prefer direct, immediate feedback. Or where another might prefer a phone call to an email. Or when still others need to spend a bit of time with you getting feedback every day.

By understanding and honouring these preferences you create an environment where people feel respected and supported, they trust you and this means your influence increases.

The power of influence in INFINITE Leadership

Influence in INFINITE Leadership is about inspiring others, building trust and creating a culture where every team member feels valued, heard and respected. An INFINITE Leader is not focused on their power over others. They're focused on psychological safety, effective communication and leading by example. The goal here is to use influence not as a way to control outcomes, but as a catalyst to unlock potential and achieve success for everyone involved.

(?) Reflection Questions

1. What steps can I take to build greater trust with those I lead, in order to strengthen my influence?

2. How do I communicate my vision to my team or organisation, and how can I improve my ability to inspire others to share and act on that vision?

3. How do I ensure that my influence stems from authenticity and integrity, rather than from authority or control?

4. Who are the people who have influenced me the most as a leader, and what traits or actions made their influence so impactful?

Our next pillar on the INFINITE Leadership journey is transformation.

'The key to influence is to first be influenced. Seek first to understand, then to be understood.'

– Stephen R Covey

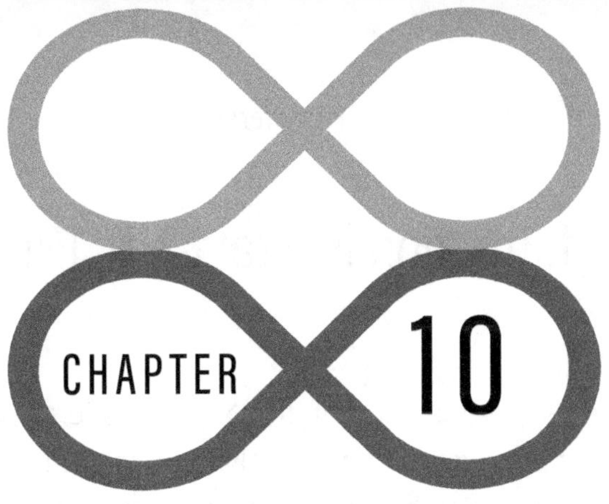

T - TRANSFORMATION

'On a path of transformation, you must be willing to give up your false beliefs and self-limiting stories.'

– Heatherash Asara

Along your INFINITE Leadership journey, transformation is the ongoing evolution of yourself, your team and even your organisation. But creating true transformation for yourself, your team and your organisation requires asking a lot of great questions, a willingness to challenge the status quo and to be open to new possibilities. It's about understanding that what got you here won't get you there.

In this chapter we'll explore why transformation matters to INFINITE Leadership, the barriers to transformation, the importance of strategic questions and how to foster a legacy of change within your organisation.

Why transformation is vital to INFINITE Leadership

Transformation is at the core of INFINITE Leadership because it empowers leaders to evolve continuously, both in their self-leadership and in how they nurture others. It is the accumulation and consolidation of the previous pillars of Identity, Nurture, Fearlessness, Innovation, Nobility and Influence. But having the pieces of the puzzle isn't enough. It's putting the different pieces of the puzzle together and watching the picture come to life in front of you. This is what creates the magic.

Personal transformation in leadership often requires deep introspection, emotional intelligence and a commitment to self-improvement, as highlighted by thinkers like Susan David, who emphasises the role of emotional agility in navigating complexity and uncertainty.[100]

Professionally, leadership transformation is about evolving the way we influence and inspire teams to ensure long-term success. This includes creating systems of feedback, developing others, and ensuring sustainability within organisations. James Kerr, in his book *Legacy*, discusses how transformational leadership is rooted in leaving a lasting impact by empowering others to succeed long after the leader is gone.[101]

At its core, transformation is what drives continuous improvement, resilience in the face of challenges and a culture that values growth, all of which are vital for INFINITE Leadership.

---

100 David. Emotional Agility.

101 Kerr, J. (2015). *Legacy: What the All Blacks Can Teach Us about the Business of Life.* Constable.

The essence of transformation

Creating genuine transformation requires more than just skills or strategy. It demands a deep level of self-awareness and the ability to reverse engineer your goals. That means that you have to begin with the end in mind, starting with understanding exactly what it is that you're working towards. First ask yourself, what's the ultimate outcome you seek? And then identify the key steps, actions and behaviours required to achieve that outcome.

Transformational work is about understanding how the steps, actions and behaviours required to lead transformation work at the intersections between purpose, people and processes. It's the process of peeling back the layers to identify what is truly needed to achieve those outcomes and ends that you've identified.

Barriers to transformation

1. Ego

One of the biggest barriers to transformation is the ego. Leaders often struggle to let go of control and worry that their significance to the team (and therefore their role!) might diminish if they're not the only ones making decisions. Letting go of this need to be the sole driver of success will open the way to transformation.

Ego, when unchecked, often leads to rigidity in thinking, limiting a leader's ability to adapt and embrace change. Leaders who are driven by ego may find it challenging to accept feedback, admit mistakes or recognise areas for improvement, which are all critical to transformative leadership.

In *Ego is the Enemy,* Ryan Holiday emphasises how ego can derail leaders by fostering complacency, arrogance and a resistance to learning. He shares the story of Howard Hughes, whose empire crumbled due to his inability to evolve and listen to those around him because he was blinded by his ego and personal insecurities.[102]

A few years ago I was working with a leadership team that wanted to update the policies and procedures of their organisation to align with current challenges and clientele. But they were really struggling and couldn't understand why it was so hard? Because the CEO was the one who initially developed those procedures and policies, she felt that the changes were an attack on her. Ultimately, her inability to see her ego was halting innovation and growth meant she lost her leadership team.

2. Lack of self-awareness

Transformation begins with understanding your own triggers, strengths and weaknesses. When we aren't self-aware, we might begin to blame others or circumstances for any lack of progress, rather than taking on responsibility for our actions and decisions. A lack of self-awareness blinds leaders to their own flaws and areas for improvement. Leaders who fail to acknowledge their limitations cannot address them, leading to stagnation in their personal development and a lack of progress in their professional leadership transformation.

Marshall Goldsmith identifies that many successful leaders hit a plateau because they are unaware of the behaviours that are holding them back.[103] Goldsmith emphasises that leaders who are not self-aware fail to recognise habits like over-assertiveness or the need for approval,

---

102   Holiday, R. (2017). *Ego is the Enemy: The Fight to Master Our Greatest Opponent.* Profile Trade.

103 Goldsmith, M. (2008). *What Got You Here Won't Get You There: How successful people become even more successful.* Profile Business.

which can prevent them from reaching their next level of success and leadership transformation.[104]

Leaders lacking this awareness can alienate their teams, lose trust and fail to inspire transformation, because their actions are out of sync with what the situation requires. I think we can all think of a leader for which this holds true.

3. Fear of change

Change is always uncomfortable, but especially when it requires us or our team to move out of the status quo and our comfort zone. But transformation is not possible without stepping into the unknown. We need to be courageous, lead by embracing change and inspire others to do the same.

I tell people that the comfort zone is poorly named. And perhaps a more appropriate name is the familiar zone. Very few people I know are actually happy, content and comfortable in the comfort zone. It is more that it is known and familiar. The idea of 'better the devil you know' can be detrimental to our growth, wellbeing and overall transformation.

4. Skills gaps

A lack of skills or capacity can hinder our transformation efforts. As a leader you will need to be able to accurately assess the skills within your decision-making team – including your own – and identify any gaps that may need filling. You're responsible for providing the training and support that will bridge those gaps and allow true transformation.

---

104 Goldsmith. What Got You Here Won't Get You There.

5. Inconsistent decision-making

As we'll see, good strategic decision-making that allows for real transformation must be balanced between a focus on the short-term and the long-term. If we only focus on short-term or quick wins, we'll find that we are making inconsistent decisions that could undermine long-term transformation. We need to be aware of how each of our choices aligns with our overall vision and goals.

Flip-flopping on decision-making, saying one thing to one person and something different to another person for fear of upsetting them, moving the goalposts or just NOT making a decision all contribute to diminishing trust and increasing uncertainty and confusion. It creates dissension in the ranks whether you are the CEO of a Fortune 500 company or a parent of multiple children.

How to become a transformational leader

To become a transformational leader we need to first start with understanding what might be holding us back, which we've now done. But now the real work begins as we must learn how to overcome those barriers and leave a lasting transformational legacy.

Start with self-reflection

As with all the steps of our INFINITE Leadership journey, we need to start with our own self-reflection. To begin, reflect on your journey as a leader. How have you personally transformed over the last few years? What events or insights triggered that transformation?

Identifying these insights or triggers can start you on the path of self-reflection, helping you to understand what drives change within yourself and what can drive and inspire change in others.

As we have learned in earlier chapters, self-reflection is not just about understanding your past. It's also about recognising the beliefs, habits, triggers (both conscious and unconscious) and even actions that may have helped you to lead transformational change, or alternatively held you back from doing so. Consider whether you're tending to avoid difficult conversations or resist delegating tasks because you might fear losing control.

By understanding your own obstacles and strengths you can begin to adopt a mindset that allows you to develop new strategies that better align with transformational change. This step is crucial to becoming a true INFINITE Leader.

Understand that legacy is the goal

The next step is to understand that creating a legacy is the goal. But that doesn't mean an ego-driven legacy. So, what is legacy in terms of your INFINITE Leadership?

In INFINITE Leadership, legacy is the lasting impact one leaves behind, the contribution to something greater than oneself that endures beyond one's own time. As we saw earlier, James Kerr emphasises that legacy is about ensuring that the standards, values and practices you build today positively shape the future.[105] It's not just about immediate success, and it's certainly not about YOUR success. But it is about creating something that continues to thrive and evolve long after you're gone.

---

105 Kerr. Legacy.

Transformation is a long game. To gain impactful, sustainable transformations we must have our 'big hairy audacious goals', as Jim Collins refers to them, in sight as well as a focus on what we need to do short term to get there. It is not an either/or. It is a both/and.

Legacy is not just what we leave behind; it's how we act every day to inspire future generations of leaders. True transformations require us to think bigger than ourselves which is why understanding legacy is so important. I remember a conversation with someone a few years ago that said they had no intention of leaving a legacy. I curiously asked if they were aware they'd leave a legacy whether they wanted to or not? And those who are conscious of this will have the greatest positive impact. If we are unconscious to this story, it is likely to be a legacy of destruction through a series of unaware actions.

Leaders are encouraged to focus on creating a lasting impact and making sure they positively influence their teams, organisations and society as a whole. Kerr challenges leaders to look beyond their time in a role and consider how their decisions and actions today will shape and benefit future generations.[106]

One of my most powerful transformations was leaving a secure government role to start my own business. How did that even happen? Well, it was because I didn't want my legacy to be staying in a role that didn't align with my true north. I didn't want my children thinking that this was the lesson – to stay, even if you are unhappy. I wanted the lesson to be, if you don't like your circumstances (personally or professionally) you have the power to change it. I wanted my legacy to be a reminder that we can reap the rewards of doing hard things. I also wanted my legacy to inspire my kids to take action and choose the actions and behaviours that will align to the goals they are seeking to accomplish.

---

106 Kerr. Legacy.

Embrace the macro to micro approach

One way that I like to approach transformation is to think about the 'macro to micro' and 'micro to macro' concepts. Macro, of course, represents the big picture vision or the overarching goal. The micro goals on the other hand are the steps or smaller actions that you need to take to enable you to achieve that goal. Often successful transformation involves reverse engineering from the macro perspective down to the micro level tasks. Steven Covey says to begin with the end in mind.[107]

A really great example of this was a client I had who wanted a promotion. Unfortunately she faced a lot of obstacles to achieving that goal because her boss considered her too valuable to the team and didn't want to let her go. She'd done such a fantastic job of creating a robust team, that now the boss felt that the team needed her.

So, in order to get released for a promotion, we had to reverse engineer what she had done to build up the team in the first place. In doing so we recognised that she needed to create some succession planning for the organisation which would give her boss confidence that the team would remain in good hands, while giving her the opportunity to reach for further goals. By reverse engineering her goal, we were able to break down the 'transformation' into manageable steps that ensured that the team was well equipped for the change.

This kind of process often feels akin to peeling back the layers of an onion. We start by identifying the desired outcome, breaking it into actionable parts and creating a plan that you can execute consistently. Some people will only require a high-level overview in order to take action. But others need it broken down into detailed, step-by-step

---

107 Habit 2: Begin With the End in Mind®. FranklinCovey. https://www.franklincovey. com/the-7-habits/habit-2/.

guidance. Your role as a transformational leader is to provide the support necessary to facilitate that change.

Another client of mine wanted a new role. They were ready for a change. First, we identified the macro, where she saw herself and what roles she was looking for and identified some key opportunities. We then backward-mapped this journey from updating her CV and selection criteria stories, to completing an audit of potential gaps in her skills (in accordance with the roles she was looking for) and created opportunities both in and out of work for her to develop these skills.

Whether it be a personal transformation involving weight loss or a professional transformation involving being promoted to a new role, having a clear vision of what you are working towards and clear steps to get there is imperative. This allows you to recalibrate in real time by making minor tweaks, rather than getting disheartened and having to start over from scratch when things aren't working.

It also allows us to celebrate the distance travelled. Albert Bandura's work on self-efficacy shows that individuals' belief in their ability to succeed is shaped by smaller successes along the way.[108] When leaders or individuals fail to acknowledge these incremental achievements, they miss out on opportunities to build confidence and resilience. If success only feels possible at the final goal, self-doubt can creep in during the process.

Close the skills gap

A critical element of transformation is being able to identify and close the skills gap within yourself and within your team, which sets the stage

---

108 Lopez-Garrido, G. (10 July 2023). 'Bandura's Self-Efficacy Theory Of Motivation In Psychology.' Simply Psychology. https://www.simplypsychology.org/self-efficacy.html.

for transformational growth and extraordinary achievements. How does this work?

Well, many people have the will to change, but lack the necessary skills. On the other hand, some people have both the will and the skill, but can still face barriers due to the lack of capacity or support. It's your job as the INFINITE Leader to assess these gaps and co-create strategies with your team members to address them.

According to research, around 70% of change programs fail to achieve their intended outcomes because they haven't accurately identified the skill gap.[109] When I think about the skills gap, I often think of the old Roadrunner and Wile E Coyote cartoons. In those cartoons, Wile E Coyote did a lot of work trying to catch the Roadrunner, but he was lacking skill. The Roadrunner had both will and skill, and so there was a gap between them where the Roadrunner was often successful and Wile E Coyote often was not.

---

109 Nohria, N & Beer, M. (2000). 'Cracking the Code of Change.' *Harvard Business Review.* https://hbr.org/2000/05/cracking-the-code-of-change.

To be INFINITE Leaders, we must identify the skills gaps correctly, and then help to fill those – whether the gap is our own, or is within our greater team.

Consider succession planning and sustainability

For transformation to be sustainable, and we certainly want it to be, as a leader we must make sure we have implemented succession planning. The risk with having a single 'champion' in the business is that when that champion leaves, usually the initiatives they've championed falter as well. INFINITE Leaders know that true transformation occurs when the ship can run even if they're not on board and trust that it will get to the destination with everything and everyone still intact. In other words, the organisation and initiatives will continue to thrive even in your absence.

This mindset requires you to let go of control and trust your team. It's not the leader's job to be a gatekeeper, and often it takes letting go to really implement good succession planning, because it means sharing knowledge, building others up and creating an environment where people are prepared to take the helm when needed.

Leaders should ask themselves, 'If I got hit by a bus tomorrow, what would happen? Have I empowered my team to carry on?'

Adam Grant highlights that a culture of continuous learning and feedback fosters growth and innovation.[110] By embedding sustainability practices into leadership, individuals avoid burnout and create systems that support long-term success.[111] Succession training is critical, as it ensures that leadership is transferable across generations, creating continuity in organisations.

Simon Sinek's work underscores that great leaders prepare others to take the reins, ensuring that transformation isn't limited to their own tenure but becomes an ongoing cycle of development.[112] Transformation is not just a one-time event. It's the continuous journey of evolving oneself and fostering growth in others, allowing leadership to transcend individual limitations and perpetuate excellence.

Succession planning is imperative in INFINITE Leadership because it ensures the continuity of leadership, preserves organisational knowledge, mitigates risk and enables the development of future leaders. It helps organisations maintain stability during transitions by identifying and grooming potential leaders well in advance. Without

---

110 Grant, A. (2021). *Think Again: The Power of Knowing What You Don't Know.* Viking.

111 (22 August 2023). 'Building a Positive Culture of Continuous Learning: Key Strategies for Organisations.' Institute of Data. https://www.institutedata.com/us/blog/build-a-culture-of-continuous-learning/.

112 Sinek. Leaders Eat Last.

a clear plan, organisations face leadership vacuums that can result in operational disruptions and declining employee morale. Research by Deloitte shows that 86% of leaders believe succession planning is an urgent priority, but only 14% feel they do it well, which puts companies at risk during unexpected leadership changes.[113]

Leadership changes can expose organisations to various risks, including loss of key relationships, cultural misalignment and performance dips. Succession planning reduces these risks by ensuring that successors are well-prepared for their roles. According to Harvard Business Review, two out of every five new CEOs fail within their first 18 months, which can be attributed to a lack of adequate succession planning and preparation.[114]

Effective succession planning encourages leadership development at all levels of the organisation. It is a strategic investment in employees, ensuring that they are given opportunities to grow, take on more responsibilities and be ready to step into leadership roles when needed. A 2019 Korn Ferry study found that companies with effective succession plans have 1.5x higher employee retention and 2x higher leadership development effectiveness.

When leaders leave without a succession plan in place, organisations lose critical institutional knowledge. Succession planning helps to retain and pass on this knowledge to future leaders, ensuring that new leaders understand the company's history, processes, and values. Research by PwC highlights that a lack of succession planning can cause

113 Rosenthal, J et al. (2018). 'The holy grail of effective leadership succession planning: How to overcome the succession planning paradox [Report].' Deloitte Insights. https://www2.deloitte.com/content/dam/insights/us/articles/4772_Leadership-succession/DI_Succession-planning.pdf.

114 Charan, R. (February 2005). 'Ending the CEO Succession Crisis.' *Harvard Business Review.* https://hbr.org/2005/02/ending-the-ceo-succession-crisis.

organisations to lose valuable knowledge and relationships, which can cost them time and money in trying to rebuild.[115]

Succession planning sends a strong message to employees that the organisation is committed to their growth and development. It fosters a culture of trust and engagement by showing that leadership opportunities are available to those who invest in their careers. Gallup reports that companies with engaged employees who see growth opportunities through succession planning have 21% higher profitability than those without.[116]

As we can see, succession planning is not just a nice to have, it is a must have. Effective leadership transitions are essential to an organisation's long-term health and stability, and research consistently shows that those with robust succession plans outperform those without. If we want to continue to transform ourselves, our teams and our organisations we must ensure we build the capacity in others to continue the transformation journey. INFINITE Leadership is not about being indispensable. It's about empowering others to take the helm, so that the ship runs just as smoothly in your absence as it does in your presence.

Make strategic decisions – balancing the short- and long-term

Another key to transformation is really understanding the psychology of decision-making. INFINITE Leaders need to understand the difference

---

115   Hoffman, T & Womack, S. (2011). 'Succession planning: What is the cost of doing it poorly… or not at all?' PwC. https://www.pwc.com/gx/en/oil-gas-energy/publications/pdfs/energy-company-succession-planning.pdf.

116   Sorenson, S. (7 January 2023). 'The Benefits of Employee Engagement.' Gallup. https://www.gallup.com/workplace/236927/employee-engagement-drives-growth.aspx.

between short- and long-term decision making and how to balance short-term actions with long-term vision.

But in order to make informed choices and decisions based on both immediate and future goals, you need to have the right information. This balance applies to all aspects of decision-making in life, whether it's weight loss, business growth or even friendships.

Your decisions as an INFINITE Leader are guided by your thoughts and feelings, which in turn, determine your actions or inactions. To avoid being a 'one-hit wonder', you need to think beyond quick wins and look for longevity in your decision-making. This is also how we build an enduring legacy.

To do that we have to understand the historical, psychological and emotional factors that influence decision-making. This brings us right back to one of the biggest barriers to transformation – and that is not being self-aware, or not understanding our own identities or triggers. And when we're not self-aware, we keep focusing on what's happening *to* us, rather than what we have choice and control over. Referring back to the identity section, and learning how to become more self-aware, will enable us to make better, more 'infinite', strategic decisions that lead to real transformation.

Our best decisions are made when we have access to effective tools, communication and data as well as the skills to utilise these, along with emotional and data literacy, critical thinking skills and resilience.

Create a safe learning environment

For true transformation to occur, there must be a safe environment for learning and growth. This provides yourself and your team with psychological safety, where individuals feel secure in taking risks and feel free to express themselves without fear of judgement or reprisal.

When I speak about psychological safety with my clients, I find that there's this overarching belief that, if they want to support the creation of excellence, organisations have the responsibility to be responsive psychologically and provide safer environments for people to work. While this is true, for true transformation to occur, we also have to take responsibility for our own part in that as well. Of course, organisations play a crucial role, but it falls on each individual to take responsibility for their part in creating that important sense of belonging.

As a leader, you must ask yourself, 'How do I create a sense of belonging and a safe learning environment for others?' But equally, you need to ask yourself, 'What do I need to feel safe as well?' And, 'Do I understand what I need in order to feel included as an individual and as a learner?'

By understanding both your own needs and those of your team, you can create a culture that supports this all-important continuous learning that can lead to transformation.

Leading the path of transformation

Transformation – as its name implies – is an ongoing journey. It requires self-awareness, commitment to growth, and courage on your part as a leader. Just as a butterfly emerges from its chrysalis, a leader who embraces change evolves from within, shedding old limitations to reveal their fullest potential. The beauty of transformation lies not just in the end result but in the courage to trust the process, embracing discomfort and uncertainty as essential parts of the journey toward something spectacular.

And it requires both you and your team to continuously evolve.

Use the reflection questions provided below to guide your journey of transformation. When you embody the change you want to see, you set the foundation for a culture that encourages others to also step into their potential and embrace their own path of transformation. So your journey as an INFINITE Leader is both a catalyst and a compass for the legacy you leave behind.

 **Reflection Questions**

1. How have you personally transformed as a leader in the last few years, and what triggered that transformation?

2. What beliefs or habits do you currently hold that might be preventing you from leading transformational change?

3. How do you ensure that your leadership vision is aligned with both your personal values and the long-term goals of your organisation?

4. How do you inspire others around you to embrace change and take ownership of their own transformation?

Now that we've covered transformation we're on to our final INFINITE pillar – ecosystem.

'Transformation is a process, not an event. It is driven by the need for a new vision and the relentless pursuit of that vision.'

– John P. Kotter, Leading Change

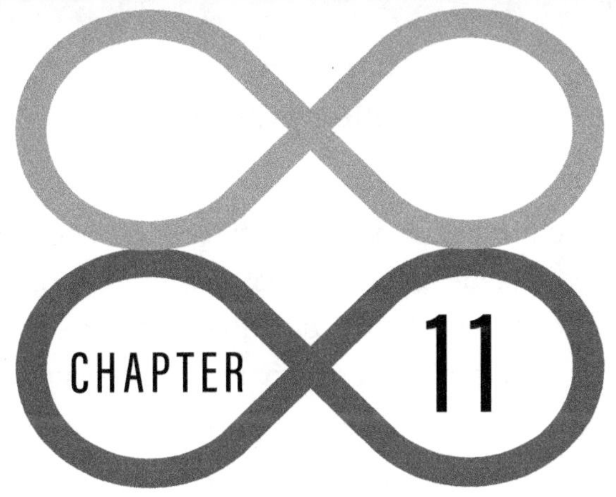

E – ECOSYSTEM

'Your network is your net worth.'

– Porter Gale

In your INFINITE Leadership journey, building a thriving ecosystem is essential. Your ecosystem is the dynamic, interconnected web of people, processes and environments that support your growth as a leader, and support the success of your team and your organisation.

But just any old ecosystem is not going to cut it – not if you want to become an INFINITE Leader. You need the *right* people, the *right* processes and the *right* environments. That leads us directly into why ecosystem matters for INFINITE Leadership.

The essence of ecosystem

What is an ecosystem? And why is it important? We are hardwired for connection, and we cannot do it alone. But as Jim Collins says, it's about having the right people on the right bus in the right position. So an ecosystem is essentially your network – the people and things that are around you in your leadership. But what makes an ecosystem unique from a network or a business strategy is that it requires true vision, and a wide lens perspective. It's a move from the 'ego-system' to the 'eco-system'.[117]

When we're true ecosystem leaders we're letting go of old patterns of thought and action, and of the need to be 'right' and instead we're leading from a place of curiosity, compassion and courage. Systems change leader Antoinette Klatzky describes this as 'leading from the edges' saying, 'It requires leading from the edges, having a sense of our impact on the whole, and letting go of the glorified idea of what statue might be raised in our honor when we reach the finish line.'[118]

Leading from the edges is pulling information and voices from the margins and seeing things with new perspectives and with a wider view. This is really the essence of the leadership ecosystem that we're looking to create as INFINITE Leaders.

What happens when you don't have control of those that you lead or those who you work with? That is, where you use the pillars in this model to support you to get the change that you need. It could also mean that if you have exhausted your skills, and nothing is changing, that maybe you need to look for something more in alignment with who you are now. If you have done the work, it is likely that you are not the same person you were at the beginning of this book. You have raised your awareness, your skills and overall functioning. So it's natural that you will evolve and that is a great thing.

---

117   Scharmer, O & Kaufer, K. (2013). Leading From the Emerging Future: From Ego-system to Eco-system Economies. Berrett Koehler Publishers.

118   Klatzky, A. (6 July 2019). 'What is Ecosystem Leadership?' *Medium*. https://medium.com/presencing-institute-blog/ecosystem-leadership-4227fd214f2.

Why ecosystem matters for INFINITE Leadership

An INFINITE Leadership ecosystem includes how leaders harmonise their personal values, professional responsibilities and the people around them to create a sustainable environment that supports growth for themselves and others. By understanding their ecosystem, INFINITE Leaders can make informed decisions and build resilience against disruptions while empowering others to do the same.

Seth Godin's concept of tribes, from his book of the same name, fits naturally into the idea of a leadership ecosystem, as it emphasises the power of communities that form around shared values, beliefs and purpose.[119] In the context of an INFINITE Leader's ecosystem, tribes represent the people and networks you attract, engage with and lead as part of your vision, that amplify the interconnectedness of individuals in support of a common goal.

At the core of *Tribes* is the idea that leadership is about connecting with a group of people who are united by shared beliefs and who are eager to follow a leader who gives them purpose and direction. In an ecosystem, your tribe becomes the supportive network that contributes to and benefits from each other's growth and success. The leader, in this case, acts as a catalyst for the tribe's development by providing vision, clarity and the inspiration to take action towards your shared purpose. Much like an ecosystem, a tribe thrives when there is mutual collaboration, support and trust.

Godin emphasises that anyone can lead a tribe, even without formal authority, by taking initiative, communicating effectively and building a sense of belonging. This fits seamlessly with the idea of an INFINITE

---

119   Godin, S. (2008). *Tribes: We Need You to Lead Us*. Portfolio.

Leader creating and nurturing a leadership ecosystem where the focus is not solely on hierarchy but on the relationships, shared purposes and collective empowerment that drive the group forward. In your ecosystem, your tribe might consist of team members, colleagues, mentors or broader networks, all contributing to a larger goal while benefiting from the collective energy of the ecosystem.

A critical component of Godin's tribes is the notion of leading through connection and trust rather than control. In your leadership ecosystem, this means fostering an environment where people are encouraged to contribute their ideas, take initiative and support each other's growth. Leaders who build tribes create spaces where innovation and diversity thrive because they trust their ecosystem to engage fully and push the group toward continuous improvement. This mirrors how a healthy ecosystem supports the ongoing growth of each of its components, relying on the unique contributions of every individual to maintain balance and momentum.

Additionally, Godin's *Tribes* also speaks to the importance of creating a sense of belonging. In an ecosystem, this means cultivating a culture where every individual feels valued and understood, contributing to a greater cause. For an INFINITE Leader, ensuring that everyone in your ecosystem feels connected to the mission and purpose of the leadership journey strengthens the bonds that hold the system together. The more connected and engaged the tribe is, the stronger and more resilient the ecosystem becomes.

Ultimately, *Tribes* reinforces the idea that leadership ecosystems are not just about structures or hierarchies but about the relationships and shared purpose that fuel long-term growth. Leaders who understand how to build and nurture tribes are better equipped to lead ecosystems that are dynamic, inclusive and capable of driving continuous improvement and innovation. By aligning the tribe's passion with the ecosystem's purpose, an INFINITE Leader can create an environment where both the tribe and the ecosystem thrive, constantly evolving to meet new challenges and opportunities.

Barriers to creating an INFINITE ecosystem

Too often I see people wearing busy as a badge of honour. You can always make more money or buy more things, but the one thing that is FINITE in this INFINITE journey is time.

One of my earliest memories is of someone telling me that people are in your life for a reason, a season or a lifetime. It allowed me to let go of the thought that someone had to do something bad for these things to end, and also that there usually is no good and bad person, just people that are walking in alignment or people that are not.

The second and harder lesson for me to learn was that people are comfortable supporting you to the level of THEIR comfort. This means that as you evolve on your INFINITE journey that some people will remove themselves from your life or, even worse, drag you back down to their comfort level. Release these people with love, and allow yourself to expand your ecosystem of support.

How to create your INFINITE ecosystem

As we are developing our ecosystem there's two key factors that we need to explore. One is how to create harmony within our ecosystem so everything can coexist. The second is how to invite the right things in.

Creating harmony in your ecosystem

One of the key aspects of your ecosystem is harmony. Life can often be a juggling act between personal and professional obligations. When life is busy, it can feel like our professional life takes over. When we have a young family, we might feel our personal life stops us from showing up how we'd like to in our professional life. So, when we find ourselves in this situation, how do we create that harmony?

You'll notice I haven't used the 'B' word – balance – and that's because, as I was navigating my own ecosystem journey, both personally and professionally, I always felt the precariousness of trying to establish this ever-elusive model of balance. It reminded me of a kid trying to balance on a seesaw. But what did resonate with me, as a music fanatic, was this concept of an orchestra that is creating a beautiful symphony.

An orchestra has many different parts – percussion, strings, brass, woodwind – and each part is essential to creating the perfect harmony. But when you listen to an orchestra you'll notice that in most performances one instrument will play solo for a little while, just like the lead guitar in a Guns and Roses song. This can be a beautiful part of any piece of music. But if a single instrument plays solo for too long, it takes away from the overall beauty and harmony of the symphony. In the same way, you can't have every instrument playing too loud, or every instrument playing too soft, or too fast or too slow. It is when every instrument comes together to create more than the sum of its parts – that's harmony.

In the same way, we need harmony in our ecosystems. So we're required to be the conductor guiding that orchestra, deciding what to focus on at any given time and maybe even coming back into the orchestra with your own instrument to add to the overall harmony being created. As leaders, you guide the pace and tone. And you continually make adjustments, allowing for solos when necessary as well, to create the ultimate harmony.

This perspective reminds us that creating a thriving ecosystem is not about achieving a single perfect balance, but about guiding the interplay of all parts to create something even more beautiful. It's also our job to remind our staff and our team to ensure they're focusing on doing this as well.

Creating harmony between your personal and professional life

Creating harmony between your personal and professional life is an important part of creating a sustainable ecosystem, but it's a dynamic process that requires continuous awareness and intentional action. This ensures that all the important people, elements and areas in your ecosystem receive the attention they need to continue to contribute to the overall harmony of your life and of course your leadership.

Start by recognising that your personal and professional lives are interconnected and are going to overlap. At times one will be more important than the other, but they must, for the most part, return to harmony quickly and easily. When one area is out of sync, it often impacts the other. For example, if you're overworking and not giving yourself enough downtime, you might find yourself struggling with burnout. It could also affect your relationships and wellbeing too. Conversely, your personal stress can spill over into your professional life – and this can lower your focus and productivity, and negatively impact your ability to lead effectively.

Instead, set boundaries that allow you to fully engage in each part of your life without letting one overshadow the other. This might mean setting limits on your work hours, prioritising self-care or scheduling time for personal and family growth.

There is a significant amount of information at the click of a button about how you can let your work and life get out of alignment, particularly when you're doing work that you perhaps don't love, or where you feel that you have to stay. But I think an under-discussed topic is how prevalent this can be when you LOVE your job as well.

I love what I do. It rarely feels like work (or what I consider to be a laborious task I have to do against my will). But the trap here is that a lot of the time I eat, sleep and breathe my work. It is a calling. And because it's a calling, I don't often give myself the downtime I need. The risk of burnout in this scenario is also significant, because you can do it all day.

Your support ecosystem is vital here. They will be the ones asking if you are taking care of yourself, prompting you to make time each day, week, month, quarter and year for yourself. They will hold you accountable in this and check in with you to remind you that you can rest and that not only is it better for you, it also ensures that you have energy for your own ecosystem, not just energy to give to others.

Gatekeeping your ecosystem

Gatekeeping is sometimes considered to be a negative thing, but in this case it's an important part of creating your ecosystem. That's because we need to be in control of who's allowed in our ecosystem.

By their nature, ecosystems are constantly evolving over time. The people who were a central part of your ecosystem years ago may no longer serve the same role. That's not to say that the friends you've had since you were five shouldn't still be an important part of your ecosystem when you're 55 – as long as they're still the right people for your journey. But what does that mean? What should you be doing to refine your ecosystem and make sure that you're surrounding yourself with the right people in the right places to support you on your INFINITE Leadership journey?

Regular auditing of your ecosystem is crucial. The practice of auditing your ecosystem is really just about taking a hard look at the energy you're getting from the people, the places, the environments and even the situations and conversations that you're surrounded by. Notice who and what is energy-giving and who and what is energy-draining. It's essential to recognise these dynamics and adjust your ecosystem accordingly. You might need to introduce new connections, join different networks or different teams, or sometimes even go to different organisations. You might also consider creating an external network that can support you with your internal growth.

My Nanna lived to just shy of her 107th birthday. One of her great passions was gardening. Whilst I did not acquire her love or skill at gardening, I learned many lessons by observing her. Tending to a garden involves nurturing the plants that are flourishing and removing weeds that could choke their growth. When she tended her garden, her weeding wasn't destructive. It was a deliberate, ongoing practice to preserve the health and vitality of the garden and it allowed the right plants to flourish and thrive.

In the same way, gatekeeping your personal and professional ecosystem allows you to identify the elements that are nourishing your growth – like supportive relationships, empowering habits, or productive processes – and continue to nurture them. It also allows you to 'pull out' the people, behaviours or commitments that can drain your energy or stifle your progress, just like weeds in a garden.

Interestingly, these weeds may not always be harmful in obvious ways, but over time, they take up space and resources, making it harder for you to flourish as an INFINITE Leader. By proactively removing these 'weeds' through mindful decisions – whether it's setting boundaries, adjusting your mindset, or letting go of unhelpful influences – you make room for what truly matters.

This process doesn't have to be harsh or brutal, and if you are walking in alignment as an INFINITE Leader it will be considered, gentle and intentional, creating space for new growth and opportunities to emerge. Just as Nanna adjusted to changing seasons and conditions, you can adapt to new phases in your leadership journey by continuously reflecting on what's nourishing or depleting your ecosystem. By protecting your energy and environment with care, your leadership garden can remain vibrant, resilient and full of potential.

You need to ensure that your leadership ecosystem is ready to support your INFINITE Leadership journey, not hold you back.

Supporting your relationships

Supporting relationships within your leadership ecosystem is essential for fostering a thriving environment where collaboration and mutual growth can flourish. To do this, active communication is crucial. Being proactive in reaching out, checking in regularly, and truly listening to those around you helps build trust and strengthens the ecosystem. By showing genuine interest in the perspectives of others, you create a space where people feel heard, respected, and valued.

Equally important is practising empathy and emotional intelligence. Understanding and responding to the emotional needs of those in your ecosystem ensures that the support you offer is meaningful. By being attuned to their challenges and emotions, you can better engage with others, while managing your own reactions in a constructive way. Strong relationships are built on this foundation of emotional understanding.

Another way to support your relationships is by fostering mutual growth. Relationships within a leadership ecosystem should never be one-sided. They should encourage learning and development for all involved. Sharing knowledge, celebrating others' successes and creating opportunities for growth ensures that the ecosystem becomes more dynamic and resilient over time. When you help others reach their potential, it strengthens the entire environment, including your own leadership journey.

At the same time, maintaining awareness and equilibrium is key. Setting clear boundaries and managing expectations is necessary to avoid burnout and ensure that relationships remain healthy. Transparency in expectations helps avoid misunderstandings and creates respect. Likewise, being a resource and advocate for the people in your ecosystem strengthens those relationships. Whether through guidance, connections or simply offering support when needed, showing up for others builds stronger, more loyal bonds that benefit the whole.

Leading by example is one of the most effective ways to support the relationships in your ecosystem. When you demonstrate the values you want to see reflected – such as integrity, accountability and authenticity – others will be inspired to follow suit. This consistency reinforces positive dynamics within the ecosystem, allowing everyone to feel more engaged. Celebrating the contributions of those around you also plays an important role. By regularly recognising and appreciating the efforts of others, you strengthen their sense of belonging and reinforce the value of collaboration.

In supporting these relationships, it's important to remain adaptable and open to feedback. Relationships evolve, and flexibility is key to sustaining them over time. When you are open to growth and willing to adapt to changing dynamics, people will feel supported, and this strengthens their connection to you. Encouraging collaboration over competition builds a sense of community that benefits everyone. Promoting synergy within your ecosystem leads to stronger collective success and enhances innovation.

Finally, investing in long-term relationships is crucial. Taking the time to nurture these connections, staying engaged and being present ensures that your leadership ecosystem is built on deep trust and resilience. Strong relationships, cultivated over time, become the foundation of a healthy and sustainable ecosystem, benefiting both your leadership and the individuals within it.

In creating your ecosystems, be aware of the type of person you want to be, and the type of people that you give permission to enter your ecosystem. In Adam Grant's *Give and Take* he identifies how to discern supporting relationships within your leadership ecosystem. He highlights how individuals approach interactions and collaboration through three main styles: givers, takers and matchers.[120]

In the context of an INFINITE leader's ecosystem, Grant's ideas offer a framework for understanding how generosity and reciprocity play crucial roles in building strong, sustainable relationships.

Givers – those who contribute to others without expecting anything in return – are often the leaders who foster the most thriving ecosystems. Their selfless acts of support and willingness to help others succeed create a culture of trust and collaboration. By giving freely, these leaders build deeper relationships based on goodwill and mutual respect, which ultimately strengthens the ecosystem as a whole.

Givers act as the 'nurturers' in the ecosystem, providing resources, mentorship and guidance that enable others to grow, while also contributing to their own development. However, to avoid burnout,

---

120 Grant, A. (2013). *Give and Take: A Revolutionary Approach to Success.* W&N.

it's essential that givers also maintain boundaries and ensure their contributions are balanced with self-care, a concept aligned with setting healthy boundaries within your ecosystem.

Takers, on the other hand, focus on what they can gain from others, often without reciprocating. In a leadership ecosystem, takers can disrupt harmony by draining resources and undermining trust. While they may achieve short-term success, their relationships tend to be transactional, which weakens the bonds that are crucial to a healthy, thriving ecosystem. Leaders who prioritise taking over giving create an environment where competition outweighs collaboration, leading to fragmentation and distrust within the ecosystem.

Matchers fall somewhere in between, aiming for an equal balance of give and take. They operate on the principle of fairness, striving to ensure that relationships are reciprocal. While matchers can build supportive relationships by ensuring equity in exchanges, their focus on tit-for-tat reciprocity may limit the potential for deeper connections that come from truly generous interactions.

In your ecosystem, matchers might be reliable contributors, but they may miss opportunities to foster the rich collaboration and innovation that come from a more giving mindset. As an INFINITE leader, embracing the giver mentality while being mindful of boundaries helps create a more supportive and vibrant leadership ecosystem. By focusing on how you can add value to others – whether through mentorship, support or sharing knowledge – you encourage a culture of mutual benefit and collaboration, which ultimately comes back to benefit the entire ecosystem, including yourself.

Ecosystems flourish when leaders prioritise giving, trust is built and a culture of shared success emerges. In this sense, giving strengthens the entire system, ensuring long-term sustainability, innovation and growth for everyone involved.

Actively seek diverse perspectives (leading from the edges)

One of the leaders I most admired was a strong female director. She didn't fall into the trap that some female leaders do, of having to 'act like a man' to make it in a male-dominated space. She was the first person who advised me not to employ in my likeness. Instead, she taught me to employ people who didn't think like me, which would help me to encourage and embrace the different perspectives they bring to the table.

It is generally easier to work with people who think like you because they just seem to 'get it'. You don't have to take the time to get everyone on the same page or think as much about your communication style. However, when you do employ people like you, it sets your ecosystem off balance and inhibits growth and innovation.

If you have developed the INFINITE Leadership mindset, you will encourage, seek and embrace people who see the world through a different lens, and by having a strong sense of psychological safety you'll also love the gifts that this brings into your own personal leadership development as well as to your team and your organisation. The goal is to challenge your thinking and continually evolve your awareness, to create INFINITE possibilities and INFINITE opportunities. Remember, if you are always the smartest person in the room, you are in the wrong room. It's time to evolve your ecosystem.

Building an ecosystem that thrives without you

As you develop your leadership ecosystem, it's a good time to remember that a truly successful one can thrive even if you, yourself, are taken out of it. Again, your role as a leader is to build a framework that encourages and supports your team to make decisions, take action and work towards shared goals. This requires careful planning and a commitment to succession and sustainability. And if your ecosystem relies solely on your presence to function, it just isn't sustainable. Instead, your aim is to create a self-sustaining network that can continue to evolve, adapt, and succeed while you 'lead from the edges'.

Reflecting on your ecosystem

As you navigate the journey of developing an INFINITE Leadership ecosystem you must always be thinking of how to keep it in harmony – and undertaking audits to fix anything that's knocked it off balance. If you're not sure if you're currently in harmony, you can start by asking yourself the following reflection questions:

 **Reflection Questions**

1. How would you describe your current leadership ecosystem? What are its strongest components, and where do you see potential gaps?

2. Who are the key people in your life and leadership journey that provide support, guidance, and growth? How do you cultivate and maintain these relationships?

3. In what ways do you create harmony between your personal and professional lives? Are there areas where one is negatively impacting the other?

4. How often do you evaluate and refresh your professional networks? Are you actively seeking diverse perspectives and feedback to strengthen your ecosystem?

Your ecosystem is important. It's the culmination of all the work that's gone on before in your INFINITE Leadership journey. And it's important because it's the dynamic space that – when carefully nurtured – creates the harmony necessary for growth, both personally and professionally.

As the conductor of your ecosystem orchestra, you need to guide the interplay of its parts and ensure each instrument (element) can be heard in the right way and at the right time. As you reflect on your journey through previous chapters remember that building an effective ecosystem requires the consistent practice of the INFINITE Leadership pillars – influence, self-awareness, transparency, integrity and nurturing. Your growth as a leader depends on your ability to adapt and build a harmonious network that supports you to thrive as a leader and your team to thrive as well.

> *'A leader is one who knows the way, goes the way, and shows the way.'*
>
> – John C Maxwell

CONCLUSION

This book has covered the many facets of the INFINITE Leadership journey, including identity, nurturing, fearlessness, innovation, nobility, influence, transformation and ecosystem – the INFINITE pillars. These pillars are designed to help you reflect on your current leadership practices and mindset and inspire you to elevate these to the next level.

The strategies and insights you've explored in this book serve as a starting point for your own INFINITE journey. As you begin to implement these concepts into your professional, and perhaps even personal, life you'll find opportunities to create that ripple effect that extends not just to your direct team but also to your organisation and even the wider community. It's important to remember that leadership is not about perfection but progress. INFINITE Leadership is about embracing a mindset that continuously evolves over time – allowing you to adapt and grow in ways that both benefit you and positively impact those around you. Continuous self-reflection is key. It's the small, consistent steps you take every day that will ultimately shape your legacy as an INFINITE Leader.

As you move forward, consider this your introduction to the stage – it's time to be the conductor of your own symphony. Be intentional about how you build and nurture your ecosystem, remain open to continuous learning, model the way for others and remember to reflect, review, and recalibrate as often as you need on your evolution to INFINITE Leadership. The journey to becoming an INFINITE Leader is ongoing – but now you have the tools and awareness to lead your orchestra (and yourself) with skill and confidence.

In his book *The Infinite Game*, Simon Sinek reminds us that sometimes we will be ahead of the game and sometimes we will be behind, but it is those that see the game as INFINITE that will always go further than they thought possible.

Getting support

One of the most important aspects of leadership is knowing where and how to get support. I often speak about the need for safe spaces where leaders can engage in brave and courageous conversations. And one of these is finding the right coach for you.

The power of coaching for leaders

One of the most profound experiences I've had, and what ultimately led me to coaching, was working with a coach myself. Over the years, I participated in various professional development programs. Some were great. And some less so. But it was coaching that truly transformed my leadership and helped me develop reflective practices. My journey of self-reflection allowed me to become the leader of my own life.

As a leader, the pressure to perform in every aspect can be overwhelming, especially when there are competing priorities. You can often feel like you're not doing anything well. But with the support of a coach you can put the systems in place that will help you navigate your leadership. This is someone who can hold space for your brave and courageous conversations as you lead yourself and others on their journey. The saying we heard earlier in the book holds true here too, 'What got you here won't get you there.'[121] That's why INFINITE Leaders need to

---

121 Goldsmith. What Got You Here Won't Get You There.

continuously reflect, evolve and recalibrate their approaches – and where GREAT coaches can really help.

Please get in touch with me to talk about any aspect of your own INFINITE Leadership journey. I'd love to hear how you get on.

Kylee

WORK WITH KYLEE

If you're ready to deepen your journey toward INFINITE Leadership, Kylee Leota is on hand to help support you on your way. With over two decades of experience in leadership development, Kylee helps individuals, teams and organisations to align their values, goals and strategies with their leadership mindset and practices in order to create lasting change. Through her programs, coaching and workshops she empowers leaders to foster environments of trust, transparency and growth, and helps organisations to see true transformation.

If you're looking to refine your leadership skills, build a thriving ecosystem or transform your team's culture, Kylee's guidance can help you with the small, consistent steps needed to achieve your big vision. Together you can build a world of INFINITE Leaders.

Work with Kylee Leota

- **Executive and Leadership Coaching:** Become an INFINITE Leader through personally designed coaching, tailored to enhance your skills and performance. This coaching can be 1:1 or group coaching for your organisation.

- **Speaking:** Keynote Presentations on becoming an INFINITE Leader. These presentations can also specifically focus on key Pillar, bespoke to your organisation to empower an INFINITE Leadership mindset.

- **INFINITE Leadership Program:** A comprehensive program designed to develop and drive a culture of continuous improvement and create excellence for everyone. Available

205

from 90 minutes to 3 full days, this program is designed to meet your organisation where it is at, to develop and empower INFINITE Leadership across your organisation.

Visit Elements4Success or get in touch with Kylee's team at:

admin@elements4success.com.au

to learn more and start your own INFINITE Leadership journey.

ACKNOWLEDGEMENTS

I never considered myself a writer, but I always loved learning. From a very young age, books were a safe space for me, whether I was wrapped up in the adventures of The Famous Five, or feeling all of my feels with Judy Blume's, characters such as Deenie, to in my later years, feeling seen as I navigated life with Elizabeth Gilbert and feeling 'finally' understood by authors such as , Brene Brown, Simon Sinek and Adam Grant. As a writer, I wanted to make people feel seen, heard and understood just as those authors had done for me. It was in education that I understood what it meant to feel empowered, first as a student, thank you in particular to Mrs Laurel Featherstone, and Mrs Rosina Tucker, for demonstrating the power of caring and nurturing and how that can have such a profound impact on a child's life. Secondly as an Educator, I saw firsthand the power of connection and the importance of believing in people, particularly when they didn't believe in themselves. Helping them become INFINITE Leaders themselves when they could see their own gifts they had to offer. I have been blessed to be a part of so many incredible young people's lives.

Writing INFINITE Leadership has been an extraordinary journey, shaped by countless conversations, lessons, and shared experiences. This book is not just the product of my thoughts, but a reflection of the wisdom, support, and encouragement of the many incredible individuals in my life.

To my family and friends, your unwavering belief in my vision has been the anchor that kept me grounded. Thank you for understanding when I went quiet when I was knee deep in my thoughts and writing and for being a sounding board for my "think out loud" consolidation of my ideas.

ACKNOWLEDGEMENTS

Thank you to my children, Chloe, Connor and Brody, for believing in me and navigating life around me getting this book finished. A huge thanks to Bosco Anthony who was an early adopter of my INFINITE idea, and a huge supporter along the way. To Mark Henderson, Samantha Rush, Dr Adam Harrison and Susanne Le Boutillier along with everyone else who have cheered me on, thank you

To my mentors and peers, your insight and encouragement have helped shape this work. You've challenged my perspectives, broadened my understanding, and fueled my desire to create something that resonates with leaders at every level. Your guidance has been invaluable, and I'm forever grateful for your inspiration. As special mention needs to go to Jane Anderson, who was the guide I needed to get me through the fog to the otherside, and actually put my ideas into book form. I am so grateful for your unwavering belief in me.

To my admin team, both past and present, who have helped my take my thoughts and make them something that can be shared with the world, Sahara Kiriona and Hannah Balba, thank you.

To my editor Kristen Lowry and publisher Sylvie Blair. Thank you for your grace and compassion as I navigated writing my first book. It certainly lit a spark in me and that is in huge part to your support (and hand holding) through this process.

To the leaders I've had the privilege of working alongside, thank you for sharing your struggles, triumphs, and insights. You've shown me what it means to lead with authenticity, to navigate change with courage, and to continuously strive for excellence. Your stories are woven into the fabric of this book. To my coaching clients, who have granted me the enormous honour and privilege of holding space for your brave and courageous work, you are so incredible.

To the readers of INFINITE Leadership, you are the reason this book exists. May these pages inspire you to explore your own identity, nurture your ecosystem, and embrace transformation with fearlessness and nobility. This journey is for you—may it serve as a guide to help you unlock your infinite potential and create excellence not only for yourself but for everyone around you.

Finally, to those who dare to dream of a better future, thank you for being a source of boundless inspiration. Together, we can create a legacy of leadership that truly knows no limits.

Love

Kylee x